CW01425464

SUCCESS IN THE YEAR OF THE RAT

[2020 EDITION]

Linda Dearsley

DARK
RIVER

Published in 2019 by Dark River, an imprint of Bennion Kearny Limited.
Copyright © Dark River 2019

ISBN: 978-1-911121-84-8

Linda Dearsley has asserted her right under the Copyright, Designs and Patents Act, 1988 to be identified as the author of this book.

All Rights Reserved. No part of this publication may be reproduced, stored in a retrieval system, or transmitted in any form or by any means, electronic, mechanical, photocopying, recording or otherwise, without the prior permission of the publisher.

This book is sold subject to the condition that it shall not, by way of trade or otherwise, be lent, re-sold, hired out or otherwise circulated without the publisher's prior consent in any form of binding or cover other than that it which it is published and without a similar condition including this condition being imposed on the subsequent purchaser.

Dark River has endeavoured to provide trademark information about all the companies and products mentioned in this book by the appropriate use of capitals. However, Dark River cannot guarantee the accuracy of this information.

Published by Dark River, Bennion Kearny Limited
6 Woodside
Churnet View Road
Oakamoor
ST10 3AE

www.BennionKearny.com

TABLE OF CONTENTS

CHAPTER 1: SUCCESS IN THE YEAR OF THE RAT

Welcome to the Year of the Rat which begins, or began, if you're on catch-up right now, on January 25 2020, and powers on through until February 11 2021.

But, as you raise a glass to toast the New Year, you might want to make sure it's filled with something a little stronger than usual – because this is not just any old New Year, this is a genuinely momentous occasion. The Year of the Rat 2020 – also known as the Year of the White Rat or the Golden Rat – could literally mark the dawn of a whole new era.

In fact, even if you've never been the type before, this might be the perfect time to start a diary, or at least keep notes, because this year we're all on the launch-pad, about to blast off in an entirely new direction – and you won't want to forget a thing.

A Fresh Start - on Steroids!

So why is 2020 so significant? It's all down to an extremely rare and fateful synchronisation of East and West.

In Chinese astrology, the centuries are divided into 12-year cycles, rather than the ten-year decades we're familiar with, in the West. And Year One of each new Chinese cycle is always the year ruled by the magical zodiac Rat.

Every New Year is welcomed as a fresh start, of course, we all love that feeling of turning to a sparkling new page and putting the past behind us. And in the West, should that New Year also usher in a brand new decade, it's even more meaningful than the mundane years in-between. Similarly, in the East, the Year of the Rat heralds the start of a whole new cycle, is seen as an exciting new beginning… times TWELVE.

Rat years always tend to blaze in with an invigorating change of energy. But in 2020, that exhilarating buzz comes supercharged.

In 2020, a Rat year and a new decade join forces, and travel together for the next 12 months – an event so rare, it's only happened once before in over 100 years. The powerful energies of both East and West converge to mark 2020 as the start of something really big – a fresh start – on steroids.

Oh, and the last time in a century this happened? That was 1960 – the incredible year that kicked off the Swinging Sixties and changed the world. The decade that started with the launch of the first communications satellite and ended with a man on the Moon.

After the White or Golden Rat swept in, in 1960, the modern era was born, and nothing was ever the same again.

2020 is shaping up to be just as momentous.

Your Chance to Reboot Your Future

So what will the Year of the Golden Rat (let's agree to call it the Golden Rat – sounds so much more enticing) bring for you? Can you expect to be showered with Golden opportunities and zoom into the new age with a glowing smile on your face, or will you have to be dragged out – protesting – into the dazzling new light? This is possibly a once in a lifetime chance to shape a glittering new future and make your dreams come true – but it's important to go about it in the right way.

Every Year is Different – from Day One

To make the most of the fantastic opportunities on offer in the Year of the Rat, you need to get your head around the Chinese way of looking at these things – which is quite different from what we're used to in the West.

Whereas, in the West, we tend to think of each New Year as anonymous and impartial – an unwritten book just waiting for events to fill the blank pages and create its theme – in Chinese astrology, it's just the opposite.

No year in Chinese astrology is ever anonymous. Each arrives bristling with its own unique animal 'personality' fully-formed and ready to rock, from day one.

In the East, the events don't influence the year – the year influences the events.

So every New Year's Day, a totally different animal energy is unleashed on the world – and if you understand the effect that energy might have, you're more likely to work out what to expect and how to benefit.

Circumstances that might have led to dangerous disputes in a fiery Tiger year could pass by with scarcely a ripple when peaceful Rabbit is running the show. A laid-back, 'eat, drink and be merry' approach might work wonders when carefree Pig is at the helm, but try it on in a conscientious Dog year, and such laziness could spell disaster. So, it really pays to know what you're dealing with.

A Burst of Energy

Last year, the partying Pig brought the previous 12-year cycle to a close, and there was a certain drifting quality in the air. People felt weary and glad of a chance to ease up, relax, and go with the flow.

But too much relaxation can lead to stagnation if it goes on too long. And that's where Rat comes in. Rat can't be doing with all that sitting around. Rat's got places to go, people to see, and is always busy, busy, busy.

Rat years arrive like a hi-energy shot in the arm, or a bucket of icy water over the head, depending on your point of view. Either way, beneficial change is unleashed.

Inspiration, creativity, and sheer movement abound. Suddenly, half-formed plans or ideas we never thought would come to anything seem achievable. We view things from a different angle and notice possibilities we'd previously overlooked.

Can-do attitudes will be rewarded.

Can't-be-bothereds will miss out.

The Glamorous Golden Rat

Yet, just like people, not all Rat years are the same. The Chinese zodiac acknowledges that while all Rat years will share the same basic Rat characteristics, there will be a subtle difference in emphasis to reflect the personality of the particular Rat in charge that year.

Zodiac Rats come in five different varieties, or breeds you might say, each with its own unique way of expressing Rat-ness. There are Water Rats, Wood Rats, Fire Rats, Earth Rats, and Metal Rats. And 2020 is the Year of the Metal Rat. Which is why it's also known as the Year of the White or Golden Rat – the colours white or gold representing the Metal element in Chinese astrology.

It's been 60 long years since the glamorous Golden Rat last shimmied over the horizon. So what was going on in 1960 that might give us a clue as to what to expect in the coming 12 months?

Meet the Golden Rat of 1960 – just beginning to Swing

Rats are masters of survival. If they get the choice, they don't make risky moves until they're sure the coast is clear. So, in 1960, as the year opened, Harold Macmillan was still Prime Minister in Britain, and Dwight Eisenhower still President of the USA.

Possibly, to most people, it must have appeared that the world would potter on in the same old familiar way. Yet, little by little, the unseen Rat energy was gathering. By February, P.M. Harold MacMillan – known as 'SuperMac' – was already sensing a stirring in the air. On a visit to Africa, he made a famous, prophetic speech: 'The wind of change is blowing...' MacMillan told his audience, '...whether we like it or not.'

He didn't realise just how right he'd prove to be. By November, across the Atlantic, the man who was to become the USA's most legendary President – the charismatic John Kennedy was elected.

JFK was to inspire the world. At home, he promised to boost government spending to end the recession then plaguing the US, to expand the space programme, and he even declared that by the end of the decade, the USA would put a man on the Moon. Few believed such a dream was possible, and although JFK didn't live to see it, that's exactly what happened.

And it wasn't just JFK who made his mark. Waiting in the wings when Kennedy was elected was his elegant wife, Jackie. Just as Rats enjoy spending money – especially on luxury items and especially within the family – so First Lady and mum of two Jackie took one look at the White House, which was to be their new home, and decided it urgently needed redecorating. Out went the dowdy, traditional furnishings, and in came Jackie's chic new style.

She didn't stop there. Photogenic Jackie had her own signature look. It involved striking bouffant hair, pink lipstick, and a series of sleek Chanel suits with boxy jackets often worn with a jaunty pill-box hat. Soon, Jackie was appearing on magazine covers around the world. It wasn't long before America's First Lady was an international fashion icon and women across the globe were backcombing their hair and clamouring for their own version of the Jackie outfit.

Busy Rat restlessness was breaking out everywhere. It was out with the old, in with the new. In South America, Brazil downgraded former capital Rio and created a fresh, purpose-built capital city in the interior of the country. Contemporary Brasilia, designed, when viewed from above, in the shape of an aeroplane, was inaugurated in April 1960.

Over in Africa, countries that had once been colonies were demanding independence, while in East Germany, the government became so alarmed at the number of citizens packing their bags and leaving for the West, they began building the infamous Berlin wall to keep them in.

Sophisticated Rome hosted the summer Olympics that year. In the UK, Princess Margaret married the photographer, Anthony Snowdon, walking up the aisle in a dazzling gown of stunning simplicity. It was the first royal wedding ever to be televised, and immediately changed the style of bridal dresses for years to come.

In London, the first traffic wardens began to patrol the streets, while in a sensational court case, the long-banned novel Lady Chatterley's Lover was ruled to be 'not obscene'. It immediately went on sale and sold 200,000 copies in one day.

In the cinemas, Spartacus – the story of a rebellious slave – was wowing audiences, and scary Psycho was just about to be released. In the dance halls, Chubby Checker was imploring teenagers to do 'The Twist', while in Liverpool, a group called the Silver Beetles accepted a stint in a Hamburg club and decided to perform under a new name: The Beatles.

Elvis Presley, meanwhile, was discharged from the army and returned home to record his biggest selling single of all time. 'It's Now or Never.'

It certainly was.

The 2020 Golden Rat

It's fair to say 1960 was quite a year. A year that set the agenda for the rest of the decade. So what will the Golden Rat bring us in 2020? Looking back, it's clear that 1960 was a year of beginnings, of events that started small and gradually grew and grew until they reverberated down the decade, having a massive impact.

Chances are 2020 will be the same. The sharp-eyed and the shrewd, endowed with typical Rat intelligence, will spot the new ventures destined for lasting success and cash in. A powerful entrepreneurial spirit will sweep the world. New businesses, new fashions, new ideas of every kind will flourish.

Rats are very sociable creatures and enjoy being part of a crowd, so entertainments involving large get-togethers will come to the fore. Festivals, parties, and group activities of every kind will attract devoted followers.

Like 1960, the 2020 Golden Rat brings us another summer Olympics – this time in the sophisticated city of Tokyo – the perfect event for a Rat year combining, as it does, large crowds having fun, competitiveness, and for the winners, a hoard of shiny metal medals to take home.

The general air of prosperity and optimism will cheer people up as Rat years are reckoned to be fortunate and times of plenty. Yet, ironically, just as climate change activists are demanding a return to a simpler way of life, Rat years inspire soaring ambition and the pursuit of material wealth.

Rat works hard to make a pile and then likes to spend it on flashy, luxurious items. No way is Rat going to forego the central heating, start walking to work, and swap a hotel holiday for a week on a campsite – so there could be some clashes with the eco-warriors this year. In fact, we could see two factions developing – with the hard-core climate activists on one side, and the hedonists on the other – ready to fight back.

Money, Money, Money

The Golden Rat brings the element of Metal to 2020, so the car industry, shipbuilding, IT, aerospace, and other industries that use metal should do well. Even better, when metal is combined with a touch of glamour such as jewellery-making or tasteful items for the home, designers and even blacksmiths could find themselves unusually in demand.

And despite Rat's aversion to roughing it, or possibly because of this, innovative alternative energy inventions will flourish and make great strides – particularly when they combine low-carbon efficiency with home comforts.

Above all, though, metal is the element of money, so we can expect banks, finance, insurance and the pursuit of profit to be major themes throughout the year.

Just don't expect Rat to be perfect.

The Rat is a bit of a gambler and has a tendency to cut corners when the going looks good. Scandals involving financial skullduggery could shock the world. Companies that are household names could collapse without warning due to unwise investments.

In fact, risk-taking – particularly with other people's money – could prove hard to resist in 2020, and whole currencies could end up in trouble. Politicians should take note.

It has to be said, too, that Rats can be aggressive at times, particularly metal Rats – all that shiny military hardware being very attractive to them. Back in 1960, the first US troops were sent to Vietnam. They had no idea it was the start of something deeply unpleasant. They were to be embroiled for years, and it didn't end well.

On a personal level, get-rich-quick schemes will abound and anyone tempted with an offer that looks too good to be true, would do well to slam the door.

The chances are that, this year, most of us will be so absorbed by our work, so busy chasing exciting new goals, we won't be as concerned with travel as usual – unless that travel is career-related. Conventional holidays may lose their appeal, but since Metal has an affinity with Water, the popularity of cruises may increase even further.

Finally, 2020 is the year of new beginnings. Chances are, ventures and events that start this year will be influencing our lives for a very long time to come.

How the Years Got their Names

According to Chinese folklore, there are many explanations as to why the calendar is divided up the way it is. Perhaps the most popular is the story about the supreme Jade Emperor who lives in heaven. He decided to name each year in honour of a different animal and decreed that a race would be run to decide which animals would be chosen, and the order in which they would appear.

Twelve animals arrived to take part. Actually, in one legend there were 13, and included the cat, at the time a great friend of the rat. But the cat was a sleepy creature and asked the rat to wake him in time for the race and in the excitement (or was it by design?) the rat forgot and dashed off leaving the cat fast asleep. The cat missed the race and missed out on getting a year dedicated to his name. Which is why cats have hated rats ever since.

Anyway, as they approached the finish line, the 12 competitors found a wide river blocking their route. The powerful Ox, a strong swimmer, plunged straight in, but the tiny Rat begged to be carried across on his back. Kindly Ox agreed, but when they reached the opposite bank, the wily Rat scampered down Ox's body, jumped off his head and shot across the finish line in first place. Which is why the Rat is the first animal of the Chinese zodiac, followed by the Ox.

The muscular Tiger, weighed down by his magnificent coat, arrived in third place, followed by the non-swimming Rabbit who'd found some rocks downstream and hopped neatly from one to another to reach dry land.

The Emperor was surprised to see the Dragon with his great wings, fly in in fifth place instead of the expected first. The Dragon explained that while high up in the sky he saw a village in flames and the people running out of their houses in great distress, so he'd made a detour and employed his rain-making skills (Chinese Dragons can create water as well as fire) to put out the blaze before returning to the race.

In sixth place came the Snake. Clever as the Rat, the Snake had wrapped himself around one of the Horse's hooves and hung on while the Horse swam the river. When the Horse climbed ashore, the Snake slithered off, so startling the Horse that it reared up in alarm, allowing the Snake to slide over the finish line ahead of him.

The Goat, Monkey, and Rooster arrived next at the river. They spotted some driftwood and rope washed up on the shore, so Monkey deftly lashed them together to make a raft and the three of them hopped aboard and floated across. The Goat jumped off first, swiftly followed by Monkey and Rooster. They found they'd beaten the Dog which was unexpected as the Dog was a good swimmer.

It turned out the Dog so enjoyed the water, he'd hung around playing in the shallows emerging only in time to come eleventh. Last of all came the Pig, not the best of swimmers and further slowed by his decision to pause for a good meal before exerting himself in the current.

And so the wheel of the zodiac was set for evermore, with the Year of the Rat beginning the cycle, followed by the Ox, Tiger, Rabbit, Dragon, Snake, Horse, Goat, Monkey, Rooster, Dog and Pig.

How to Succeed in 2020

So, since 2020 is the Year of the Rat, how will you fare? Does the Rat present your astrological animal with opportunities or challenges? As the fable about how the years got their names shows, every one of the astrological animals is resourceful in its own special way. Faced with the daunting prospect of crossing the river, each successfully made it to the other side, even the creatures that could barely swim.

So whether your year animal gets on easily with the Metal Rat, or whether they have to work at their relationship, you can make 2020 a wonderful year to remember.

Chinese Astrology has been likened to a weather forecast. Once you know whether you need your umbrella or your suntan lotion, you can set out with confidence and enjoy the trip.

Find Your Chinese Astrology Sign

To find your Chinese sign just look up your birth year in the table below.

Important note: if you were born in January or February, check the dates of the New Year very carefully. The Chinese New Year follows the lunar calendar and the beginning and end dates are not fixed, but vary each year. If you were born before mid-February, your animal sign might actually be the sign of the previous year. For example, 1980 was the year of the Monkey but the Chinese New Year began on February 16 so a person born in January or early February 1980 would belong to the year before – the year of the Goat.

And there's more to it than that...

In case you're saying to yourself, but surely, how can every person born in the same 365 days have the same personality(?) – you're quite right. The birth year is only the beginning.

Your birth year reflects the way others see you and your basic characteristics, but your month and time of birth are also ruled by the celestial animals – probably different animals from the one that dominates your birth year. The personalities of these other animals modify and add talents to those you acquired with your birth year creature.

The 1920s

5 February 1924 – 24 January 1925 | RAT

25 January 1925 – 12 February 1926 | OX

13 February 1926 – 1 February 1927 | TIGER

2 February 1927 – 22 January 1928 | RABBIT

23 January 1928 – 9 February 1929 | DRAGON

10 February 1929 – 29 January 1930 | SNAKE

The 1930s

30 January 1930 – 16 February 1931 | HORSE

17 February 1931 – 5 February 1932 | GOAT

6 February 1932 – 25 January 1933 | MONKEY

26 January 1933 – 13 February 1934 | ROOSTER

14 February 1934 – 3 February 1935 | DOG

4 February 1935 – 23 January 1936 | PIG

24 January 1936 – 10 February 1937 | RAT

11 February 1937 – 30 January 1938 | OX

31 January 1938 – 18 February 1939 | TIGER

19 February 1939 – 7 February 1940 | RABBIT

The 1940s

8 February 1940 – 26 January 1941 | DRAGON

27 January 1941 – 14 February 1942 | SNAKE

15 February 1942 – 4 February 1943 | HORSE

5 February 1943 – 24 January 1944 | GOAT

25 January 1944 – 12 February 1945 | MONKEY

13 February 1945 – 1 February 1946 | ROOSTER

2 February 1946 – 21 January 1947 | DOG

22 January 1947 – 9 February 1948 | PIG

10 February 1948 – 28 January 1949 | RAT

29 January 1949 – 16 February 1950 | OX

The 1950s

17 February 1950 – 5 February 1951 | TIGER

6 February 1951 – 26 January 1952 | RABBIT

27 January 1952 – 13 February 1953 | DRAGON

14 February 1953 – 2 February 1954 | SNAKE

3 February 1954 – 23 January 1955 | HORSE

24 January 1955 – 11 February 1956 | GOAT

12 February 1956 – 30 January 1957 | MONKEY

31 January 1957 – 17 February 1958 | ROOSTER

18 February 1958 – 7 February 1959 | DOG

8 February 1959 – 27 January 1960 | PIG

The 1960s

28 January 1960 – 14 February 1961 | RAT

15 February 1961 – 4 February 1962 | OX

5 February 1962 – 24 January 1963 | TIGER

25 January 1963 – 12 February 1964 | RABBIT

13 February 1964 – 1 February 1965 | DRAGON

2 February 1965 – 20 January 1966 | SNAKE

21 January 1966 – 8 February 1967 | HORSE

9 February 1967 – 29 January 1968 | GOAT

30 January 1968 – 16 February 1969 | MONKEY

17 February 1969 – 5 February 1970 | ROOSTER

The 1970s

6 February 1970 – 26 January 1971 | DOG

27 January 1971 – 14 February 1972 | PIG

15 February 1972 – 2 February 1973 | RAT

3 February 1973 – 22 January 1974 | OX

23 January 1974 – 10 February 1975 | TIGER

11 February 1975 – 30 January 1976 | RABBIT

31 January 1976 – 17 February 1977 | DRAGON

18 February 1977 – 6 February 1978 | SNAKE

7 February 1978 – 27 January 1979 | HORSE

28 January 1979 – 15 February 1980 | GOAT

The 1980s

16 February 1980 – 4 February 1981 | MONKEY

5 February 1981 – 24 January 1982 | ROOSTER

25 January 1982 – 12 February 1983 | DOG

13 February 1983 – 1 February 1984 | PIG

2 February 1984 – 19 February 1985 | RAT

20 February 1985 – 8 February 1986 | OX

9 February 1986 – 28 January 1987 | TIGER

29 January 1987 – 16 February 1988 | RABBIT

17 February 1988 – 5 February 1989 | DRAGON

6 February 1989 – 26 January 1990 | SNAKE

The 1990s

27 January 1990 – 14 February 1991 | HORSE

15 February 1991 – 3 February 1992 | GOAT

4 February 1992 – 22 January 1993 | MONKEY

23 January 1993 – 9 February 1994 | ROOSTER

10 February 1994 – 30 January 1995 | DOG

31 January 1995 – 18 February 1996 | PIG

19 February 1996 – 7 February 1997 | RAT

8 February 1997 – 27 January 1998 | OX

28 January 1998 – 5 February 1999 | TIGER

6 February 1999 – 4 February 2000 | RABBIT

The 2000s

5 February 2000 – 23 January 2001 | DRAGON

24 January 2001 – 11 February 2002 | SNAKE

12 February 2002 – 31 January 2003 | HORSE

1 February 2003 – 21 January 2004 | GOAT

22 January 2004 – 8 February 2005 | MONKEY

9 February 2005 – 28 January 2006 | ROOSTER

29 January 2006 – 17 February 2007 | DOG

18 February 2007 – 6 February 2008 | PIG

7 February 2008 – 25 January 2009 | RAT

26 January 2009 – 13 February 2010 | OX

The 2010s

14 February 2010 – 2 February 2011 | TIGER

3 February 2011 – 22 January 2012 | RABBIT

23 January 2012 – 9 February 2013 | DRAGON

10 February 2013 – 30 January 2014 | SNAKE

31 January 2014 – 18 February 2015 | HORSE

19 February 2015 – 7 February 2016 | GOAT

8 February 2016 – 27 January 2017 | MONKEY

28 January 2017 – 15 February 2018 | ROOSTER

16 February 2018 – 4 February 2019 | DOG

5 February 2019 – 24 January 2020 | PIG

The 2020s

25 January 2020 – 11 February 2021 | RAT

12 February 2021 – 31 January 2022 | OX

1 February 2022 – 21 January 2023 | TIGER

22 January 2023 – 9 February 2024 | RABBIT

10 February 2024 – 28 January 2025 | DRAGON

29 January 2025 – 16 February 2026 | SNAKE

17 February 2026 – 5 February 2027 | HORSE

6 February 2027 – 25 January 2028 | GOAT

26 January 2028 – 12 February 2029 | MONKEY

13 February 2029 – 2 February 2030 | ROOSTER

CHAPTER 2: THE RAT

鼠

Rat Years

5 February 1924 – 24 January 1925

24 January 1936 – 10 February 1937

10 February 1948 – 28 January 1949

28 January 1960 – 14 February 1961

15 February 1972 – 2 February 1973

2 February 1984 – 19 February 1985

19 February 1996 – 7 February 1997

7 February 2008 – 25 January 2009

25 January 2020 – 11 February 2021

Natural Element: Water

Will 2020 be a Golden year for Rats?

Congratulations Rat! 2020 is your year. After more than a decade of putting up with other signs running the show – you've finally got the chance to be in charge. Your paws are grasping the levers of power and, for the next 12 months, we'll all be doing things *your* way.

Those sensitive Rat whiskers are probably already picking up hints of an exciting change in the wind. 2020 promises to be awesome for you.

As the zodiac Rat always heralds the start of a new cycle, most Rats will be buzzing with brilliant ideas, desperate to shake off the sluggish, why-rush vibes of 2019's year of the Pig, and leap into action.

Yes, this time next year you really could be millionaires!

But hang on a minute. Oddly enough, according to Chinese tradition, the celestial animal that rules the year isn't automatically guaranteed a completely trouble-free 12 months.

Think of it like this; you probably don't remember your first year of life. It was undoubtedly beneficial for you and it was a time when you built the foundations of everything that came after. You would have had your share of triumphs, from charming your adults into taking care of you to mastering the art of staggering across the room and finding your mouth with a spoon. But you'd have had your share of tumbles too. That was the only way to learn.

Likewise, when your celestial animal birth year comes round again, it's a time of massive opportunity, but also of making important changes and learning new lessons – which can sometimes be difficult. And there's more. Being in charge carries with it responsibility as well as fun. Like it, or not, other signs will look to you to lead the way and help them out if they don't quite understand the Rat style of doing things that will dominate this year.

Wise Rats will curb their impatience and give assistance gracefully when asked. The Rats that also take on a little charity work in some form, or make a few compassionate donations, will also store up some particularly good Karma this year.

Rats are hardworking and very good at making money and the Golden Rat, in a Metal year, could accelerate this process and shower you with cash in the coming months. You really could get rich before you have to hand over to the next animal in the cycle – the Ox of 2021 since you ask.

Self-employed and business Rats, and Rats that work in metal-related industries, will do particularly well, as will the bright sparks who start a new venture this year.

Making money is fun for the typical Rat and there will be plenty of chances to spend it too – which is also a pleasure. So what's not to like so far?

The possible pitfalls lie in overconfidence. With things going so well, many a Rat will be tempted to over-reach themselves and take on too many projects. And being so busy, they may not have time to check the small print. Slapdash work and falling victim to scams could ruin the fortunes of overly-ambitious or careless Rats.

Despite all this, Rats are set to be even more popular than usual this year. Everyone wants the charismatic Rat at their event in 2020 – partly because they're good company, but also because the other signs sense where the power lies this year.

This is great news for sociable Rats who adore dressing up and going to a good party, but they need to watch their spending on networking. Despite all the cash pouring their way, some Rats could be tempted to entertain so lavishly they end up in debt. What's more, the Rat lifestyle looks so enviable to certain other signs this year, they could find themselves the target of thieves. Rats would be well-advised to take special care of their valuables in 2020 and make sure the insurance is up to date.

As Rat enjoys the wonderful feeling of expansion this year, the idea of moving to grander premises may start to appeal. Yet, oddly enough, not so many will actually make the move. Chances are most Rats will be too busy to contemplate such a time-consuming business as packing up their home and relocating. They will very much enjoy viewing all sorts of tempting and wildly expensive properties online, of course, but will probably put an actual move on the back-burner until next year.

Finally, with career, business, and socialising being so hectic in 2020, Rats need to pace themselves and watch their health. Even the toughest of Rats can overdo it.

What it Means to Be a Rat

It doesn't sound so good does it, to call yourself a Rat? In fact, it may seem strange to start the astrological cycle with such a controversial creature as the unwelcome rodent. Here in the West, we haven't a good word to say about them. We talk of 'plagues' of rats; they 'infest' dirty, derelict places; they hang around dustbins.

They're associated with disease, rubbish, and sewers, and if a rat should be spied near our homes, we'd be straight on the phone to pest control. They make us shudder. Describe a person as 'a rat' and you're certainly not paying them a compliment.

Yet the Chinese view things differently. When they think of the zodiac Rat, they're thinking not of the flea-ridden rodent with the disconcerting long, hairless tail. They're imagining a certain energy, certain admirable qualities they associate with the creature. Rats, after all, are a very successful species. They are great survivors; they're quick, intelligent, tenacious, and they seem to thrive almost anywhere, under any conditions. All excellent qualities to be commended, if you found them in a human.

So, far from being an unfortunate sign, being born in the year of the Rat is regarded as a good omen.

Rats possess great charm and elegance. They're chatty, intelligent, and make friends easily. At parties, people seem drawn to them. There's something about their genuine enjoyment of being surrounded by new faces that makes them easy to get along with. Yet, they value old friends too, will make an effort to stay in touch, and a friendship with a rat is likely to last a lifetime.

Both male and female rats always look good. They believe that outward appearances are important. Instinctively, they understand that you only get one chance to make a first impression, so they take care never to be caught off guard looking a mess.

This happy knack is easier for them than most because they love shopping and are Olympic-standard bargain hunters. They can't resist a sale and if it's a designer outlet, so much the better. Their homes are usually equally smart for the same reason. Rats have innate good taste and are as thrilled with finding a stylish chair, or piece of artwork at half price, as they are a pair of shoes.

They enjoy spending money and the challenge of hunting down the best deal; and because they're also successful at work, they tend to have plenty of cash to splurge. Yet, despite this, Rats can often be viewed as a bit stingy. They're not mean, it's just that Rats' strong survival instincts lead them to prioritise themselves and their family when it comes to allocating their resources. Within their families, Rats are extremely generous.

Rats also enjoy the finer things in life. They prefer not to get their hands dirty if at all possible and are experts at getting other people to do the mundane tasks for them. They like pampering and luxury and lavish holidays. Yet, being supremely adaptable, they will happily embark on a backpacking trip if it takes them where they want to go and there's no other option. They're adventurous, and hate to be bored, so they're prepared to take a calculated risk if some place or person catches their eye.

Yet, this willingness to take a risk combined with the love of a bargain can occasionally get them into trouble, despite their super-sensitive survival instincts. Rats, particularly male Rats, have to guard against the urge to gamble. The combination of the prospect of winning easy money, the excitement of the element of chance, and the challenge of pitting their wits against the odds can prove irresistible. What starts as a mild flirtation for fun can end up as quite a problem.

The same could be said for suspect 'get-rich-quick' schemes. Though clever and sceptical enough to see through them, Rats are so thrilled by the idea of an easy gain, the temptation to cast doubts aside, against their better judgement, can be overwhelming.

But if any sign can get away with such unwise habits, it's probably the Rat. Rats are good at making money and at handling money. They're also masters at spotting an escape route and scuttling away down it if the going gets too tough. Underneath that gregarious bonhomie, there's a shrewd, observant brain that misses nothing. Rats have very sharp eyes and are highly observant even when they don't appear to be taking any notice. They are also very ambitious, though they tend to keep it quiet. Dazzled by their genuine charm and witty conversation, people often fail to see that most moves Rats make are taking them methodically to the top. It's no accident they call it 'the rat race'.

Best Jobs for Rats in 2020

Financial Consultant

Mortgage Advisor

Banking

Lawyer

Interior Design

Manager of any kind

Sales of Luxury Items

Event organiser

Perfect Partners 2020

Cupid's arrow can strike anywhere at any time, of course, but once the novelty of new romance wears off, some relationships are easier to maintain than others. Here's a guide to the Rat's compatibility with other signs.

Rat with Rat

These two are certainly on the same wavelength and share many interests. When their eyes first meet, passionate sparks may fly. This relationship could work very well, though over time the competitive and ambitious nature of both partners could see them pulling in different directions. What's more, if one should succumb to a weakness for gambling or risky business ventures while the other does not, it will end in tears.

Rat with Ox

Oddly enough, this combination can be surprisingly successful. Frenetic Rat and calm Ox may seem to be opposites but, in fact, Rat can find Ox's laid-back approach strangely soothing. Ox is not interested in competing with Rat and will put up with Rat's scurrying after new schemes with patience. As long as Rat doesn't get bored and has enough excitement in other areas of life, this relationship could be very contented.

Rat with Tiger

The magnificent Tiger will always catch Rat's eye because Rat loves beautiful things, but Tiger's natural element is fire and Rat's is water and fire and water don't mix well. Tiger's not interested in Rat's latest bargain, and Rat doesn't share Tiger's passion for changing the world, yet the attraction is strong. If Rat makes an effort to step back and not get in Tiger's way, they could reach a good understanding.

Rat with Rabbit

Rat finds Rabbit intriguing. Here is an attractive, stylish creature that doesn't feel the need to be pushy or take centre stage yet somehow manages to be at the heart of things. The Rat wants to find out more, while Rabbit is flattered and entertained by witty Rat's attention. These two respect each other but, over the long-term, Rat could be too overpowering.

Rat with Dragon

This couple is usually regarded as a very good match. They have much in common being action-loving, excitement-seeking personalities who hate to be bored. It takes a lot to dazzle Rat, but the Dragon's glamorous aura proves irresistible, while Dragon loves to be admired, so each enjoys being with the other. There could be the odd power struggle as these two are both strong characters, but the magnetism is so powerful they usually kiss and make up.

Rat with Snake

The Snake shares Rat's good taste and being elegant, sophisticated, and smart will delight Rat at first sight. These two get on very well on an intellectual level but perhaps are better as good friends rather than long-term partners. The Snake's love of basking in the sun for hours strikes Rat as lazy and dull, while Rat's need to rush around doing deals and meeting people seems pointless and wearying to the Snake.

Rat with Horse

Rat and Horse both fizz with energy and they love action and looking good, yet this is not seen as an ideal partnership. Nothing's impossible, of course, but these two will have to work hard to find harmony. The Rat will admire Horse's enthusiasm and cheerful approach but become impatient to discover Horse can also be fiery and emotional. Horse, on the other hand, can find Rat's risk-taking behaviour extremely worrying.

Rat with Goat

The Rat is charmed by carefree Goat and fascinated by its artistic talent and happy knack of living in the present. Easy-going Goat tends to like everyone so is perfectly content to enjoy Rat's company. These two can get along fine, yet they don't really understand each other deep down. Long-term, the Rat may find Goat's lack of interest in the practical side of life, such as finances and bills, irritating.

Rat with Monkey

Unlikely as it might appear, mischievous Monkey and the clever Rat make a good partnership. Their quick minds, sociable natures, and love of novelty ensure that they're never bored together. True, Rat might sometimes feel Monkey is too inclined to skim over the surface of things and could do with being more serious at times, but Monkey's ingenuity and audaciousness always save the day. Both can have a weakness for gambling though, so need to take care.

Rat with Rooster

The first thing Rat notices about the Rooster is its beautiful plumage, but this a relationship which is unlikely to get much further than initial admiration. Rooster's direct and frank approach can strike the Rat as tactless, while the Rooster can't understand why Rat has to make life so convoluted and complicated. Then again, Rooster's natural confidence and aplomb can come across as bragging to the Rat. These two have to be very determined to make a partnership work.

Rat with Dog

The Rat and the Dog get along pretty well together. Both are strong characters, and they respect each other and give each other space when required. But deep down, the Dog is a worrier and gets anxious about unnecessary risks, while Rat just can't help sailing close to the wind if an interesting opportunity presents itself. Long-term, reckless Rat might unintentionally drive Dog to distraction. Only to be considered by Dogs with nerves of steel.

Rat with Pig

It's very easy for Rat to be beguiled by the Pig. Pig's easy-going, sympathetic nature immediately relaxes the Rat. What's more, Pig loves shopping as much as Rat so the two of them could enjoy many happy expeditions together. Conflict could occur through overspending. Pig does not understand Rat's compulsion to bag a bargain. Pig will buy at whatever the price and the two could Love

Rat Love 2020 Style

There's good news, and not so good news, for the Rat's love life in 2020. The good news, Rat, is that it's up to you. But that's the bad news, too! Why? Because you're so thrilled with all the career opportunities and money-making schemes enticing you to stay at work just a little bit longer, chances are you'll spare little time for romance.

Single Rats will scarcely notice. Which is a shame because while you're always quite a catch, this year you're red hot. As Lord or Lady of 2020, potential partners are drawn to you irresistibly. You stand out in any crowd and could have your pick of lovers.

Yet, if you're not careful, you'll look at all those eager faces and see only networking opportunities. Should you go so far as to start a romance, you may have to cancel so many dates because of work commitments the relationship fizzles out before it's begun.

Avoid this trap, Rat, and you could actually find the ONE in 2020.

Rats already in relationships have the same problem. In fact, they may be even more careless of their partner and take them for granted. Neglecting to make time for a loved one could prove to be a big mistake. Envious eyes on the Rat's fortunate lifestyle don't just covet Rat property – they may have designs on the Rat's partner too. Spend too long away, Rat, and your other half may be stolen.

Resolve to do things differently, Rat, and this could be a wonderful year for the two of you. Treat your partner to some luxury breaks, spare some time for wining and dining, and you could be happier than you've ever been.

Secret of Success in 2020

On one level, just turning up in 2020 will bring you a measure of success, Rat, because it really is a good year for you. However, there are many ways you could shoot yourself in the foot, so it's worth taking some time to plan and curb your natural instinct to dash in and get as much done as possible, in the shortest conceivable time.

This year, more than most, you will profit from rationing your energy and your commitments. You can afford to be choosy. There are so many opportunities on offer for you. Resist the temptation to be greedy. You really can't make a good job of them all, so select a few that interest you the most and give them your full attention.

One annoying Rat fault is a tendency to skim over some of the details or fail to finish a project properly. Admit this to yourself and resolve to be disciplined. Check, recheck, slow down, and make sure you're completely satisfied before you move on.

Finally, schedule in plenty of rest. Workaholic Rats can burn themselves out before they reach the heights. You're not indestructible even though you're born under the sign of the great survivor.

Plan, adopt a disciplined approach, look after your health, and success is yours.

The Rat Year at a Glance

January – Don't be dismayed at a slow start. Your year is powering up. Patience.

February – A big investment looks interesting but tread warily. Wait a while before committing.

March – Things are looking up. Your career is rolling. You're getting noticed.

April – Busy, busy, busy. Just the way you like it. So much to do and you're having fun too.

May – Cash is flowing in like water. Metal years attract real water too, so watch out when swimming or boating.

June – Quarrelsome types may cross your path. Bite your lip and refuse to be riled.

July – Summer's arrived and, after all the hard work, it's the perfect time for a break.

August – You're doing so well envious eyes are looking your way. Watch out for false friends.

September – A change of plan is necessary. Act fast and you'll profit.

October – Career's going well but you may have to choose between two schemes.

November – Make time for love. Romance is looking for you.

December – This is the Rat's own month. Enjoy a fabulous time.

Lucky Colours for 2020: Red and yellow

Lucky Numbers for 2020: 2, 3

CHAPTER 3: THE OX

牛

Ox Years

25 January 1925 – 12 February 1926

11 February 1937 – 30 January 1938

29 January 1949 – 16 February 1950

15 February 1961 – 4 February 1962

3 February 1973 – 22 January 1974

20 February 1985 – 8 February 1986

8 February 1997 – 27 January 1998

26 January 2009 – 13 February 2010

12 February 2021 – 31 January 2022

Natural Element: Water

Will 2020 be a Golden year for the Ox?

Well Ox – if you're typical of your sign, you're probably breathing a sigh of relief to see the back of 2019 and the Year of the Pig. Though the easy-going Pig and the patient Ox are not outwardly antagonistic to each other, a quiet friction can build up between them and this has probably been reflected in the mounting number of irritations and frustrations many an Ox has encountered over the last 12 months.

If that sounds like you, break out the celebratory beverage of your choice right now because 2020 brings a huge improvement. In fact, chances are, you're going to love it!

The good news is that while being very different in character, the Rat and the Ox get on surprisingly well together. They both share the element of water which makes them creative but in complementary rather than competitive ways – so you can expect life to become easier; minor bumps in the road become much smoother than in the past.

What's more, this is a Golden Rat year, emphasising the element of metal. This suits Ox particularly well because metal is traditionally believed to be nurturing and helpful to water in Chinese astrology.

Where the last two years, which were ruled by the element of earth, could have left you bogged down, and unable to make the progress you craved, at last you're pulling free of the mire.

All those imaginative ideas and schemes Ox has been thinking about, and possibly started to develop, can finally get off the ground.

Projects in which you might have almost lost hope – might even have abandoned altogether – could unexpectedly spark into vibrant life and zoom to the heights with astonishing speed, taking everybody, including you, by surprise.

In fact, Ox – often regarded as the craftsman of the zodiac – could find their work leads to fame and fortune this year, particularly if it involves producing beautiful things by hand.

Already many Ox will have found themselves feeling more relaxed than they've been for a long time. Despite regarding themselves as completely down-to-earth, the truth is that Ox have very acute senses. This year, if you're typical of your sign, you may even find yourself surprisingly open to flashes of psychic inspiration; at the very least, you're sensing the welcome change in your luck.

Happily this has a beneficial effect on your health too, and as you let the stress slip away you'll feel better and better.

You may find the speed at which Rat operates a little unsettling and you may suspect that, at times, Rat doesn't play by the rules which makes you uncomfortable. Yet, despite this, the general air of good fortune surrounding you allows you to overlook such excesses and go about your business in your own chosen way.

Last year, there could have been occasions when the Ox career took a slight down-turn. You may have believed the boss was disappointed in some way. Perhaps this was your imagination, perhaps it wasn't, but whatever the situation – it won't be repeated in 2020.

This year, Ox efforts will receive the appreciation they deserve. Promotion or a pay rise, or both, are quite likely in 2020. Watch out too for the appearance of an ally or mentor who is going to promote your interests in a very helpful way.

This person – who could be a colleague or an authority figure – will become a great friend and continue to be an important influence in your life for years to come.

In fact, even though the Ox is not a natural party animal, you could find this new friend tempts you out and about more than usual. Even more surprising, once you've been coaxed onto the social scene, you could find you're enjoying yourself more than you thought possible.

Chances to make money and boost your bank balance will flood into your life in 2020, Ox, so be ready to grab them with both hands. And, being a sensible creature, you'll make sure you save a good chunk for less fortunate years.

Finally, the Ox is a compassionate, helpful sign, and this year someone (or possibly more than one person) will come to you for assistance. You're always willing to do what you can, but – in an unexpected way – helping this person will eventually end up helping you.

What it Means to Be an Ox

Okay, so hands up everyone who's secretly disappointed to be an astrological Ox?

Sounds a bit bovine and boring doesn't it? The Ox might lack the glamour of the Tiger or the Dragon. It can't even boast the intriguing notoriety of a sign like the Rat or the Snake. In fact, here in the West, we may not even be entirely sure what an Ox looks like. Some sort of large cow perhaps?

At first sight, you might be excused for thinking the Ox was dull. Yet, in China, that wasn't the perception at all. There was a very good reason the Ox was so highly placed – at number two – on the zodiac wheel.

The animal was revered as essential to country life. So precious, it was regarded as a gift from the Gods. So special, in fact, it's said that in the past the Chinese didn't eat beef. They couldn't possibly disrespect such an important beast by serving it up for dinner.

So, while the Ox may not seem as exciting as some of the other celestial animals, the sign of the Ox is respected and appreciated.

What the Chinese valued was the phenomenal strength and endurance of the Ox. Get an Ox moving and it will plod on mile after mile, covering huge distances with apparent ease and without complaint. Without the work of the Ox, many a family would have gone hungry.

People born in the year of the zodiac Ox are believed to be blessed with similar qualities. For this reason, though unflashy and quietly spoken, they often end up being extremely successful in whatever they undertake

– from their career to their favourite hobby, or creating a harmonious family that blossoms.

Ox have a wonderful knack of planning a sensible, logical course to wherever they want to go and then following it, relentlessly, step by step until they get there, no matter what obstacles they encounter en-route. Oxen find it rather puzzling that other people can't seem to adopt the same simple approach. They don't understand why some signs give up before reaching their goal. Why do they waste their time chopping and changing and getting nowhere, wonders the Ox.

Ox patience is legendary. They may not be quick, or nimble, but they realise that slow, steady, consistent effort achieves far more in the long run. And the Ox is only interested in the long haul. At heart, the Ox is serious-minded and, though they enjoy a joke as much as anyone else, they regard frivolity as a pleasant diversion, not an end in itself.

Ox people are usually good-looking in a healthy, wholesome way but they're not impressed by flashy, passing whims and fashions. Superficial gloss has no appeal. The Ox woman is unlikely to be found rocking extreme, designer clothes or wafting fingers iridescent with the latest nail polish.

Ox tastes tend to be classic and practical. They are instinctively private and hate to draw attention to themselves, yet the Ox is one of the nicest signs. Genuinely honest, kind, and sincere, Ox is ready to help anyone in trouble, happily pitching in to lend a hand without expecting anything in return. Yet, since Ox tends to speak only when they have something to say, other signs can find them difficult to get to know. It's worthwhile making the effort because the Ox will be a loyal friend forever.

What's more, when they do have something to say, Ox views can be surprisingly frank. Just because they are patient and kind, it doesn't mean they can be pushed around. The Ox is self-reliant and makes up its own mind; it's not swayed by the opinions of others. What's more, they can be very stubborn. When the Ox finally makes a decision, it sees no reason to change it.

Ox people are not materialistic. They work hard because the task interests them, or because they can see it needs to be done, and they will keep going until the project is complete. They are the true craftsmen of the zodiac, excelling in working with their hands and they can be unexpectedly artistic and innovative when the occasion demands. As a result, money can accumulate and Ox is not averse to spending it on some creature comforts. The Ox home will be warm and styled for comfort and practicality rather than cutting-edge design. If there's no space for a garden, it's likely to be filled with houseplants too, because Ox has green fingers and needs to see nature close at hand.

Travel and holidays are not top of the Ox agenda; they enjoy their work and their home and are not forever itching to get away. Unlike many signs, they cope with routine very well. And for all their modesty and quiet diligence, there is always something impressive about the Ox. Other signs sense the latent strength and power that lies just below the surface and tend not to impose too much. This is just as well because though the Ox may appear calm, placid and slow to anger, when they do finally lose their temper, it can be terrifying. What's more, the Ox will never forget an insult and can bear a grudge for years. Ox doesn't stay mad – they get even.

Best Jobs for Ox 2020

Farmer

Horticulture; Florist, Gardener, Botanist

Garden Designer

Carer

Accountant

Potter or Craft Worker of some kind

Jeweller

Surveyor

Perfect Partners

Cupid's arrow can strike anywhere at any time, of course, but once the novelty of new romance wears off, some relationships are easier to maintain than others. Here's a guide to the Ox's compatibility with other signs.

Ox with Ox

These two could be very happy together, as long as one of them plucks up the courage to admit they're interested. Sloppy, sentimental romance is not their style and they both share this view so there'll be no misunderstandings around Valentine's Day. They know that still waters run deep and they can enjoy great contentment without showy declarations of love.

Ox with Tiger

Not an easy match. Ox and Tiger could be on different planets. Fiery Tiger doesn't frighten Ox and Tiger may admire Ox's strong, good looks and sincere nature but they both need different things from life. Tiger wants to dash about changing the world for the better, while Ox reckons you get more done by buckling down where you happen to be and attending to the details. Clashes could abound.

Ox with Rabbit

Ox finds Rabbit rather cute and appealing. Whether male or female there's something about Rabbit's inner fluffiness that brings out Ox's highly developed protective instincts. Rabbit meanwhile loves the Ox's reassuring presence and the sense of security Ox provides. These two could get on very well together as long as refined Rabbit can overlook Ox's occasional down-to-earth – Rabbit might say 'coarse' - observations.

Ox with Dragon

Chalk and cheese though this pair may appear to be there's a certain fascination between them. Ox may not approve of Dragon's showy manner but recognises Dragon's good intentions, while Dragon admires Ox's strength of character and gift for completing tasks. If each could find a way to tolerate the other's wildly different lifestyles, they might be good for each other, but long term, Dragon's hectic pace might wear even the Ox's legendary stamina.

Ox with Snake

Like Ox, the Snake is quietly ambitious and not given to racing around unless it's absolutely necessary. Ox on the other hand respects Snake's clever brain and understated elegance. These two could quickly discover how beneficial an alliance between them would be. They're both happy to give the other space when required but also step in with support when needed. This could be a very successful match.

Ox with Horse

Long ago on many Western farms, Ox was replaced by the Horse and it maybe that Ox has never forgotten and never forgiven. At any rate, these two, despite both being big, strong animals are not usually friends. Horse is too flighty and frivolous to interest Ox for long, while Ox's methodical, careful ways will irritate the Horse. Best not to go there.

Ox with Goat

Though these two share artistic natures even if in the case of the Ox, they're well hidden, deep down they don't 'get' one another. Ox may be beguiled at first by Goat's friendly, easy-going manner but then disappointed to discover Goat seems to find everyone equally delightful, even those who're plainly unworthy. Goat on the other hand can't understand why Ox won't lighten up more. This relationship would require a lot of effort and compromise.

Ox with Monkey

The naughty Monkey scandalises Ox but in such an amusing way Ox can't help laughing. Monkey on the other hand is equally amused to find an audience so easy to shock. This unlikely pair enjoy each other's company and get on surprisingly well. Yet right from the start it's probably obvious to both that a long term relationship couldn't last. A fun flirtation though could be a terrific tonic for them both.

Ox with Rooster

For all its bravado and showing off, the Rooster is a down-to-earth type, drawn to security and accumulating the good things in life – requirements that Ox understands very well and can supply effortlessly. What's more, Ox can't help but admire Rooster's fine feathers and skill at communicating in a crowd – attributes Ox doesn't have and is unlikely to acquire. These two could enjoy a very good partnership.

Ox with Dog

These two ought to get along well as they're both sensible, down to earth, loyal and hardworking and in tune with each other's basic beliefs. And yet, somehow they don't. Dog has a playful streak and finds this lacking in Ox, while Ox may be baffled by what seems like pointless silliness in Dog. If they can agree to differ they could make a relationship work.

Ox with Pig

Delightful Pig will catch Ox's eye and since Pig isn't a constant thrill-seeker, the two of them could enjoy many peaceful evenings together perhaps over a tasty meal. Yet Pig's spendthrift ways – at least in Ox's eyes, could soon prove very annoying as well as illogical to the Ox, while Pig could find Ox's attitude judgemental and upsetting. Not ideal for the long term.

Ox with Rat

Oddly enough, this combination can be surprisingly successful. Frenetic Rat and calm Ox may seem to be opposites, but in fact Rat can find Ox's laid-back approach strangely soothing. Ox is not interested in competing with Rat and will patiently put up with Rat's scurrying after new schemes. As long as Rat doesn't get bored and generates enough excitement in other areas of life, this relationship could be very contented.

Ox Love 2020 Style

Ox often pretends to be the down-to-earth type in love, and it's true that Ox's sometimes tactless way of telling the truth (as Ox sees it) can at times torpedo many a promising relationship. Yet, beneath that blunt exterior, is a surprisingly romantic heart.

Loyal, sincere, and picky, Ox affections are not given lightly; but when Ox admires someone, they tend to put them on a pedestal and worship them from afar.

If you're a single Ox, and even if you're not – this year you could fall head over heels. Passionate and devoted you may even feel a little obsessive about this new love. As long as you don't set your sights too high, and you don't overwhelm them with attention too soon, this could work out well. It could even lead to wedding bells.

Attached Oxen are not immune from falling for someone else this year. And that new someone may not be single. Complications could abound! If you want to avoid a drama, shower your partner with affection and put as much effort into your relationship as you do your work and hobbies.

Secrets of Success in 2020

You're all set to have a wonderfully successful year, Ox. You've got luck on your side, you've got influential friends, and if you work for someone else even the boss is well disposed towards you this year.

The only thing that could hold you back is your own painstaking approach. Usually, this is an asset and it's not that you should abandon your careful ways this year. It's just that all that checking, rechecking and attention to detail can slow you down, and in a Rat year events move at a phenomenal pace.

You won't be short of opportunities in 2020, but while you study one in forensic detail, there's a danger that six more will pass you by before you even notice, and someone else will snatch them from under your nose.

This is not the way you like to work, but if you resist the temptation to dig your heels in with a 'my way or the highway' approach, and ponder how you could streamline your methods and speed up your output, the sky's the limit.

Lastly, don't forget to take a break. Even if you don't feel you need one, someone close to you could. Do yourselves both a favour and have a holiday.

The Ox Year At a glance

January – A busy month but take some time to plan and streamline.

February – Your new methods are getting noticed. Keep doing what you're doing.

March – Someone has their eye on you. Is it the boss or an admirer?

April – A friend could do with a helping hand. Be kind but don't let them drain you.

May – A fiery colleague may cause a misunderstanding. Keep calm and smooth things over.

June – You're feeling unexpectedly restless. Get out of doors as much as possible.

July – Time for that holiday you've been promising you'd take. You love the water but don't overdo it.

August – Everyone else is on holiday but an unusual opportunity beckons.

September – Fine tuning is needed on a project but this is where you excel.

October – Stick with what you know is right. A colleague will support you.

November – You can afford to ease up now. Relax and enjoy.

December – Time to haul all that cash to the bank and give yourself a big pat on the back.

Lucky Colours for 2020: Blue, Yellow, Green

Lucky Numbers for 2020: 1, 4

CHAPTER 4: THE TIGER

虎

Tiger Years

13 February 1926 – 1 February 1927

31 January 1938 – 18 February 1939

17 February 1950 – 5 February 1951

5 February 1962 – 24 January 1963

23 January 1974 – 10 February 1975

9 February 1986 – 28 January 1987

28 January 1998 – 5 February 1999

14 February 2010 – 2 February 2011

1 February 2022 – 21 January 2023

Natural Element: Wood

Will 2020 be a Golden Year for the Tiger?

Good news, Tiger. 2020 looks like the year when you could really make your mark.

Unlike a lot of signs, the past two years have been a little easier for you than most. Okay, so you've had your ups and downs but others have fared a lot worse.

The Year of the Rat is set to be good for you, but in a different way from the last 24 months. In fact, it's quite possible you're going to find

2020 far more satisfying because you finally get the chance to unleash your inner Tiger, swish your tail, and make things happen.

While Rat and Tiger are not the very best of besties, they both have a healthy respect for each other which allows the Tiger to flourish in a Rat year.

Suddenly, you'll be aware of a rush of dynamic Rat energy and the urge to leap up and get things done. Yet, while the Rat uses this impulse to develop business and commerce, Tiger is more likely to be fired up with the desire to return to idealistic Tiger roots and change the world. Or rather, save the world, as Tiger might put it.

If you're typical of your sign, you've never been the materialistic type. Not that you'd turn down a pay rise if it came your way, but you're too concerned with the unfairness of the system and the suffering of the poor, or the animals, to devote too much time to chasing wealth for the sake of it.

In 2020, Tigers will be filled with the compulsion to put their careers on hold while they devote their attention to a good cause. Whether it's campaigning about climate change, saving the Koala Bears, planting trees, or aiding refugees, Tiger will be at the forefront.

Tigers who already work in the charity sector, conservation, or similar, may be in line for promotion this year, but Tigers in other fields will be content to tread water career-wise while they concentrate on worthier matters.

Ironically enough, this attitude won't harm Tiger's long-term prospects at all. This is because the Rat is a water animal, while Tiger belongs to the wood element. Water is believed to nurture wood so the Rat will look on Tiger's altruistic passions with indulgence.

As long as the Tiger goes about these humanitarian or green goals with business-like seriousness, Rat will be supportive. Give in to a little cub-type frivolity or rebelliousness – as Tiger sometimes does – and it will be a different story.

There's quite a bit of travel on offer for Tigers this year, too. It may be connected to whatever cause Tiger has adopted, or it may be a number of private trips, but either way the restless Tiger will love it.

A change of location can't be ruled out either. Whether at home or at work, the Tiger could feel the need to expand or make substantial changes. Suddenly, the longing for a new view from the window could prove irresistible, though Tiger companions may find this baffling.

Some Tigers may even decide to retrain or embark on a course of study that appears to turn their lives upside-down. If this is you – don't worry. It looks as if it will be a success.

Finally, the typical Tiger won't be particularly bothered about pursuing wealth in 2020, and it's unlikely to be a major problem for most. It looks as if past efforts or economies will be rewarded this year, so you can afford to take your paw off the accelerator for a while, and follow your heart.

What it Means to Be a Tiger in 2020

It's a wonderful thing to be a Tiger. Who could not be impressed with the great cat's magnificent striped coat, lithe yet powerful body, and arrogant, swaggering stride? We're all in awe of the Tiger – as well as being pretty scared, too.

In China, the sign is regarded as fortunate and noble. Fortunate because – let's face it – the Tiger owns the jungle and patrols his territory with savage grace; noble because it's believed the Tiger only kills when it's hungry or threatened. (Which may or may not be strictly true.)

Yet the zodiac Tiger is also a contrary creature. You never know quite where you are with the typical Tiger. With a coat neither black nor orange – neither light nor dark – Tigers have two sides to their characters and can switch moods in an instant.

What's more, that striped pelt provides such perfect camouflage in the jungle, Tiger can melt into the shadows and become completely invisible, only to reappear without warning when least expected, to devastating effect.

Other signs instinctively know never to underestimate the Tiger.

Perhaps unsurprisingly, people born under this sign tend to attract good luck. They throw themselves into risky situations and escape unscathed where others would come badly unstuck.

Tigers are fearless and restless. They like to be on the move and get bored easily. Wonderfully good-looking, Tigers tend to shine in company and enjoy being surrounded by admirers, as they usually are. While perfectly happy in their own company and not craving attention, Tigers are confident and unfazed by a crowd. They take it as quite natural that other signs seek them out and want to hear their opinions.

The Tiger has a magnetic personality and can be highly entertaining, but they're also surprisingly moody – laughing and joking one minute then flying into a rage over almost nothing the next. Despite this, the Tiger is very idealistic. Tiger can see what's wrong with the world and wants to put it right. What's more, courageous Tiger is quite prepared to get out there and put the necessary changes into action.

This is the sign of the daring revolutionary. The trouble is, Tigers can become so accustomed to getting away with audacious acts, they forget that – deep down – they're big cats and cats are said to have only nine lives. Push their luck too far and, sooner or later, Tiger can find it runs out.

Sporty and athletic, Tigers love to travel and when they're young, the typical Tiger is likely to want to be off to see the world. Even older Tigers insist on regular holidays and would happily take a sabbatical or 'adult gap year' if possible. Luxury travel or budget breaks, they don't really care as long as they're going somewhere different. They don't even mind going on their own if necessary, as they're independent and self-assured; they are confident they'll find an interesting companion from time to time, along the way, if they need one.

Far too individual to be slaves to fashion, Tigers of both sexes still manage to look stylish and original in a pared-down, sleek sort of way. They can't be bothered with fiddly, fussy details, and they don't need to be because their natural features attract attention effortlessly. Similarly, the Tiger's home is attractive and unusual: full of intriguing objects and trophies that Tiger has collected during their adventures.

At work, if they manage to avoid quarrelling with the boss and walking out – a strong possibility as Tigers hate to be told what to do – Tigers tend to rise to the top of whatever field they happen to be in. But contradictory to the end, the Tiger is just as likely to reach the peak of their profession and then resign to try something new. In business, the Tiger can be creative, innovative, and utterly ruthless to competitors.

Best Jobs for Tiger in 2020

Heading a Charity

Actor

Environmentalist

Campaigner

Freedom Fighter

Barrister

Politician

Perfect Partners

Cupid's arrow can strike anywhere at any time, of course, but once the novelty of new romance wears off, some relationships are easier to maintain than others. Here's a guide to the Ox's compatibility with other signs.

Tiger with Tiger

The attraction between these two beautiful people is powerful. They understand each other so well it's almost like looking in a mirror. They both like to walk on the wild side and will enjoy some exciting adventures together but their moody interludes could lead to fierce quarrels. This match could be compulsive but stormy.

Tiger with Rabbit

Surprisingly, the Rabbit is not intimidated by Tiger's dangerous aura and this attitude immediately appeals to Tiger who enjoys a challenge. Rabbit's calm presence and clever way with words keeps Tiger interested, while Rabbit finds Tiger's adventurous tales entertaining. With care, these two could get on well together for years.

Tiger with Dragon

The two biggest personalities in the zodiac would seem bound to clash. After all, these larger than life characters share so many similarities there's a danger they'd compete. Yet a relationship between the Tiger and Dragon often works very well. They understand each other's impulsive natures but they're also different enough to supply the support the other needs. They'd make a formidable power couple.

Tiger with Snake

Not the best of romances. These two are so fundamentally different that any initial attraction is unlikely to last. Snake likes to bask and conserve energy while Tiger wants to leap right in and race about. Tiger takes in the big picture in a glance and is off to the next challenge while Snake likes to pause, delve beneath the surface, and consider. It wouldn't take long before these two annoy each other.

Tiger with Horse

This athletic pair get on pretty well. They both like physical pursuits, testing their strength out of doors or just enjoying the feel of the wind in their hair and the ground under their feet. True, Horse may not quite understand Tiger's plans for world domination but it doesn't really matter. Horse is happy to be loyal to such a charismatic partner. As they're both moody, there could be rows but making up is exciting.

Tiger with Goat

Tiger and Goat don't have a lot in common. While their aims and temperaments are quite different, they are both sociable creatures and Goat wouldn't mind Tiger attracting all the attention when they're out together. Tiger, in return, would appreciate Goat's lack of jealousy and generosity of spirit. Yet long-term they're likely to drift apart as they follow their different interests.

Tiger with Monkey

Tiger can't help being intrigued by sparkling Monkey and Monkey is flattered by such interest. Who wouldn't enjoy being admired by such a fabulous creature? But irrepressible Monkey just can't help teasing and being teased is not a sensation Tiger is familiar with, nor appreciates. Unless the attraction is very strong, these two will wind each other up until they can bear it no longer and part.

Tiger with Rooster

The only feathered creature in the zodiac, the opulence and novelty of Rooster's appearance will draw Tiger like a magnet. What's more, deep down they are both quite serious-minded types so, on one level, they'll have much to share. Yet, despite this, they're not really on the same wavelength and misunderstandings will keep recurring. Could be hard work.

Tiger with Dog

While not exactly opposites, these two are different enough to intrigue each other yet similar enough in basic outlook to get on well. Both Tiger and Dog are idealistic and uninterested in material gain yet where Dog can be nervous, Tiger's bold; and where Tiger attracts controversy, Dog will be loyal. This partnership could be lasting and valuable.

Tiger with Pig

Carefree Pig will love to bask in Tiger's impressive aura, while Tiger will feel good about protecting this charming but unworldly creature. They enjoy each other's company and Tiger, so focused on lofty matters will find Pig's compulsive shopping too trivial to worry about. This couple could do well together as long as Pig's fondness for cosy nights in doesn't make Tiger feel trapped.

Tiger with Rat

Sleek and clever Rat can easily attract Tiger's attention because the intelligent Tiger loves witty conversation. Yet these two are not natural partners. Tiger's not interested in Rat's latest bargain and has no wish to talk about it while Rat doesn't share Tiger's passion for changing the world. Still, if they can agree to step back and not get in each other's way, they could reach a good understanding.

Tiger with Ox

Not an easy match. Ox and Tiger could be on different planets. Fiery Tiger doesn't frighten Ox and Tiger may admire Ox's strong, good looks and sincere nature but they both need different things from life. Tiger wants to dash about creating big changes, while Ox reckons you get more done by buckling down where you happen to be and attending to the details. Clashes could abound.

Tiger Love 2020 Style

Single Tigers are on the prowl again this year. With a great deal of travel in store for many big cats, the opportunities for meeting a variety of exciting new partners has never been higher.

If you're involved in charitable work of any kind, or just doing good in some way, that loving feeling is likely to rub off on the people around you, and attraction can spring up in an instant. Lightning romances will spark, possibly within hours but are likely to fade away just as quickly.

Yet, ironically, those Tigers who really would like to settle down this year are likely to find love with someone they already know. Take a fresh look at an old friend or colleague – they could be a little in love with you already, and you've never noticed.

Attached Tigers are always in danger of feeling bored, particularly if their partner doesn't share their need for variety and change. Many Tigers will find an excuse to part this year but if you want to keep the relationship going, consider working together on a joint project. Not necessarily as a career, but in your spare time. Raise money for a local hospice, train for the London Marathon in aid of charity, rent an allotment and grow organic vegetables for the homeless. Whatever interests the pair of you, do it together and your bond will grow.

Secrets of Success

Oddly enough, it's not success you're after this year Tiger – or at least, not success as other signs would define it. Most people equate success with wealth and maybe fame or status.

Such worldly matters are not so tempting for the Tiger in 2020. The new decade finds you in your most idealistic mood. This year, you want to change things for the better. You have a strong impulse to make a difference and to right wrongs – and in a measurable way too. So, success for Tigers in 2020 represents visible progress or improvement, in whatever cause you happen to be championing.

It's quite possible you will achieve this aim. In fact, you could even end up making a name for yourself, Tiger, despite having no intention of finding fame.

Just be careful you don't end up on the front pages for the wrong reasons! The trouble is, typical Tigers are completely fearless. You tend to roar in where other signs hesitate and you can put yourself in danger – quite needlessly.

Since Tiger is also a lucky sign, you get away with it more often than not. But, never forget (as mentioned above, and reiterated here), even the most fortunate cat only has nine lives.

Then there is Tiger's tendency to come over all cub-like and unpredictable from time to time. After an intense spell of effort, seriousness and single-minded devotion, Tiger suddenly has an urge to play. There's nothing wrong with letting off steam where appropriate, of course, but rebellious Tiger refuses to be restrained by other signs' ideas of what constitutes appropriate behaviour.

Tiger's idea of a little harmless, well-earned fun, can strike other signs as irresponsible. Tiger couldn't care less, of course, but it won't seem so funny when important supporters back off and withdraw assistance.

Yet the Tigers who manage to curb their impulsiveness, adopt a more cautious approach, and double check things before letting their hair down, will have a memorable and worthwhile year.

The Tiger Year at a Glance

January – Not so fast Tiger. Ideas are piling up. You can't tackle them all at once. Make a plan.

February – This is Tiger month. Now's the time to head for the jungle and make things happen.

March – Projects are shaping up nicely but a little finesse could work wonders. Fine-tune a promising scheme.

April – Things are going well but a tricky character needs careful handling. Make an effort to sweet talk them.

May – Watch out for a woman who may not be quite what she seems. Could prove draining.

June – Wide open spaces and the great outdoors are appealing. Either take a break or try to move your work into the open air.

July – Busy, busy, busy. So much to do. Pace yourself.

August – Colleagues are on holiday so you can review your progress. You've come a long way.

September – Misunderstandings crop up, yet cash is coming your way. Keep your cool.

October – A helpful boost will lift a project. Don't take all the credit – be generous.

November – You're on a roll. Things are ticking over nicely. You can afford to ease up and party.

December – Everyone else is partying and you've got a smile on your face, yet a new idea inspires you. You're ready to start again...

Lucky Colours for 2020: Grey, pink, white

Lucky Numbers for 2020: 4, 7

CHAPTER 5: THE RABBIT

兔

Rabbit Years

2 February 1927 – 22 January 1928

19 February 1939 – 7 February 1940

6 February 1951 – 26 January 1952

25 January 1963 – 12 February 1964

11 February 1975 – 30 January 1976

29 January 1987 – 16 February 1988

6 February 1999 – 4 February 2000

3 February 2011 – 22 January 2012

22 January 2023 – 9 February 2024

Natural Element: Wood

Will 2020 be a Golden Year for the Rabbit?

Well, Rabbit, this could be just the sort of year you like best. As a tasteful, sensitive type, excess is not your style. So while 2020 may not be spectacular, it will bring you steady progress in the balanced way you appreciate, without too many nerve-racking extremes to stress you out.

For many signs, last year's Year of the Pig was a kind of celestial full-stop. It was very much the end of the cycle and they saw their projects and various issues brought to a close, leaving them ready and free to embark on a new direction this year.

Unusually, it seems for the Rabbit this was not the case. Something you began last year will have a big impact in 2020 and will continue affecting your fortunes throughout the year, and possibly on into the next as well. It looks like many Rabbits made a wise choice back then, that will bring them good luck in the coming months.

For this reason, typical Rabbits won't be swept away by a bewildering stream of brand new possibilities but will instead relish developing and enhancing something of interest from last year.

Despite this, the Year of the Rat can be a little complicated for Rabbits. Rat and Rabbit respect each other and seldom fall out, yet they don't truly understand each other.

It may even be that Rabbit gets indignant with Rat, but Rat never notices – which is even more frustrating for the elegant bobtail.

The reason for this is that Rat is a water sign and Rabbit belongs to the Wood element. Water is believed to nurture and nourish Wood, so the Rat is ready and eager to help the Wood signs. But while the other two Wood creatures – the confident, couldn't-care-less Tiger, and the exuberant, up-for-anything Dragon – are strong, powerful types who accept Rat assistance as if from an old friend, and continue on their way, Rat regards the softer, gentler Rabbit as in need of special protection.

This is well meant, but Rat can come across like a nagging, over-protective mother – pushing Rabbit on and forcing the pace in a way Rabbit finds annoying and uncomfortable.

Rabbits could find themselves overwhelmed with more work than they appreciate in 2020. It's for their own good, of course, but they'd prefer to be the judge of that… thank you very much.

You may find yourself getting more irritable than usual because of this, Rabbit, but if you can keep calm and refuse to get riled, you'll see the benefit in the long-run, particularly when you take a look at your bank balance.

What's more, since the Rat is a sociable creature that loves being part of a crowd, you'll find that involving your colleagues will smoothe your path in a wonderful way. There's no need to struggle on, alone, when deluged with tasks. The right person will always appear to help if you let them. In fact, working with other people in any capacity is likely to be particularly fortunate this year.

The Golden Rat represents the metal element, of course, and metal makes Wood creatures tense – suggesting as it does sharp, cutting objects such as axes. Yet, since metal also represents money, Rabbits are likely to enjoy a boost in their wealth this year, though it may arise from circumstances that Rabbit finds a little stressful.

This would be the ideal moment to pay off any old debts. Resist the temptation to invest in anything risky, and stash the Rabbit hoard in safe savings.

Many Rabbits will be inspired to expand their careers by studying for further qualifications in 2020. This is an excellent idea. The motherly Rat will be right behind you, encouraging you onwards, and boosting your chances of success. Just don't be tempted to skive off, or abandon the course, or there'll be trouble.

Finally, this is a particularly happy year at home. When work is getting a little too hot for comfort, Rabbit can escape back to the burrow and bask in appreciation and understanding.

What's more, with all the extra cash flowing in, most Rabbits can spend blissful hours choosing exquisite new items to enjoy in their sanctuary.

What it Means to be a Rabbit in 2020

We all love Rabbits don't we? After the possibly dubious Rat, dull Ox and terrifying Tiger, the soft and pretty Rabbit seems like a welcome relief. We can all relate to the Rabbit. Big brown eyes, powder puff-tail, cute little quivering nose, and an endearing way of hopping neatly around – nobody could take offence at the Rabbit.

In fact, nobody could feel threatened by the Rabbit in any way unless they happen to be a carrot, or a salad vegetable.

Yet, in the West, not all zodiac Rabbits are proud of their sign. They believe it suggests vulnerability and lack of drive. In the East, however, the Rabbit is appreciated for some very important qualities.

Like the Rat, Rabbits are brilliant survivors; they thrive and colonise in all manner of difficult terrains; but, unlike the Rat, they manage to do this – mostly – without enraging or disgusting anyone, bar a few irritated farmers.

For all their cuddly looks, these are tough little creatures, frequently under-estimated. It's no accident that in the Chinese calendar, the defenceless, non-swimming Rabbit still manages to cross the river in fourth place, way ahead of stronger, abler creatures with seemingly much more going for them.

People born under this sign are never flashy or loud. Enter a crowded room and the Rabbit wouldn't be the first person you notice. Yet, after a while, a stylish, immaculately-turned-out character would draw your eye. Classy and understated with perfect hair and graceful gestures – the typical Rabbit. This effortlessly polished aura is a gift. A Rabbit can emerge soaked to the skin from a rainstorm in a muddy field and within minutes appear clean, unruffled, and co-ordinated. Even Rabbits don't know how they do it. They're not even aware they *are* doing it.

Rabbits are refined with cultured tastes. They love beautiful things and art of all kinds, and hate to be surrounded by untidiness and disorder. Harmony is very important to the Rabbit – both visually and emotionally. People born in Rabbit years are sensitive in every way. They hate loud noises, loud voices, heavy traffic, and general ugliness. Quarrels can actually make them ill.

Yet this loathing of discord doesn't mean the Rabbit retires from the world. Rabbits somehow manage to end up near the centre of the action and tend to walk away with what they want, without appearing to have made any visible effort to get it.

Softly-spoken Rabbits are natural diplomats. Discreet and tactful, they can always find the right words, the perfect solutions to keep everybody happy. In fact, their powers of persuasion are so sophisticated that people usually do what Rabbit wants in the belief it's their own idea. This approach is so successful that Rabbit can't understand why other signs resort to argument and challenge, when so much more can be achieved through quiet conversation and compromise.

Rabbits tend to be brilliant strategists. When other egos get too distracted, jockeying for position and trying to be in charge for the task in hand, Rabbit deftly assesses the situation and has a plan worked out before the others have even agreed an agenda. Outwardly modest, Rabbits rarely admit to being ambitious so they often end up being underestimated. Yet, privately, Rabbits can be single-minded and determined; even ruthless at times. These qualities, combined with their diplomatic skills and calm efficiency, seem to propel them smoothly to the top of whatever profession they've chosen.

Rabbits love their homes, which naturally are as beautiful and harmonious as they are. Home is a sanctuary and Rabbits take a lot of pleasure in choosing just the right pieces and décor to make their special place perfect, but in a comfortable way. Tidiness comes easily to them and they can bring order to chaos quickly and neatly with the minimum of fuss. They enjoy entertaining – preferably small, informal gatherings of good friends – and they make wonderful hosts. Since they are such agreeable types, they're popular with everyone and a Rabbit's invitation to dinner is accepted with eagerness.

When life is calm and secure, the Rabbit is perfectly happy to stay in one place. These types are not desperate for novelty though they do enjoy a relaxing holiday. Extreme sports are unlikely to appeal but gentle exercise in beautiful surroundings soothes their nerves, and if they can take in an art gallery or a historic church followed by a delicious meal, they'd be truly contented bunnies.

Best Jobs for Rabbit 2020

Diplomat

Political Advisor

Civil Servant

Beauty Therapist

Interior Designer

Hairstylist

Personal Shopper

Graphic Designer

The Antiques Business

Perfect Partners

Cupid's arrow can strike anywhere at any time, of course, but once the novelty of new romance wears off, some relationships are easier to maintain than others. Here's a guide to the Rabbit's compatibility with other signs.

Rabbit with Rabbit

These two gorgeous creatures look like they're made for each other. Their relationship will always be calm, peaceful, and unruffled and it goes without saying that their home could grace a glossy magazine. Yet though they never argue, the willingness of both partners to compromise could end up with neither ever quite doing what they want. Ultimately, they may find the spark goes out.

Rabbit with Dragon

Dragon is such a larger than life character Rabbit could feel overwhelmed at times. Also, the Dragon can be rather noisy and over-dramatic which would get on Rabbit's nerves. Yet they each admire the other's good points. If they could live next door to each other instead of under the same roof, a long-term relationship might work.

Rabbit with Snake

This subtle pair could make a good combination. They both understand the value of working behind the scenes and neither has any desire to wear themselves out on endless adventures. They share a love of art, fine things, and quiet pleasures, and they both enjoy an orderly home. These two could settle down very happily together.

Rabbit with Horse

This could be tricky. It's fairly unlikely that Horse and Rabbit would ever end up on a date but if they did, and there was a strong attraction, it could lead to a love/hate relationship. Rabbit's neat and tidy ways would enrage Horse and Horse's unpredictable moods and over-the-top reactions would annoy Rabbit. Soon, Horse is likely to bolt for the hills or Rabbit retreat to its burrow.

Rabbit with Goat

Happy-go-lucky Goat is very appealing to Rabbit, particularly as deep down Rabbit is a bit of a worrier. They're both sociable without needing to be the centre of attention and would be happy to people-watch for hours and then cheerfully compare notes afterwards. Goat is tolerant of Rabbit's need for some regular alone time to recharge too, so this couple could be a successful match.

Rabbit with Monkey

Mercurial Monkey doesn't really 'get' Rabbit. The Monkey can appreciate how well Rabbit operates and sees this approach gets good results, but it's all too picky and slow for Monkey. Rabbit, on the other hand, is amused by Monkey's quick wit and clever ways but deplores Monkey's slapdash, sometimes devious tactics. Very unlikely to work out.

Rabbit with Rooster

Another difficult match. However unfair it seems, Rooster comes over as loud, boastful, and uncouth to Rabbit while Rabbit appears dull, staid, and insufficiently admiring of Rooster's fine feathers to appeal to Rooster. These two just can't see below the surface of the other, and it would be surprising if they ended up together. Only to be considered by the very determined.

Rabbit with Dog

Despite the fact that in the outside world Rabbit could easily end up as Dog's dinner, the astrological pair get on surprisingly well. Dog appreciates Rabbit's careful, efficient ways and soft voice, while Rabbit admires Dog's energy and good intentions. Dog's lack of interest in the finer points of interior design might try Rabbit's patience, but with a little work these two could reach an understanding.

Rabbit with Pig

Pig is not quite as interested in fine dining as Rabbit being as happy to scoff a burger as a Cordon Bleu creation, but their shared love of the good things in life makes these two happy companions. Once again, Pig's spending habits might irritate Rabbit, but not too much as Rabbit is quite willing to splurge on lovely things for the home. A relationship would work well.

Rabbit with Rat

Rat finds Rabbit intriguing. Here is an attractive, stylish creature that doesn't feel the need to be pushy or take centre stage yet somehow manages to be at the heart of things, while Rabbit is flattered and entertained by witty Rat's attention. These two respect each other but long-term, Rat could be too overpowering unless they both agree to give each other space.

Rabbit with Ox

Ox finds Rabbit rather cute and appealing. Whether male or female there's something about Rabbit's inner fluffiness that brings out Ox's highly-developed protective instincts. Rabbit meanwhile loves the Ox's reassuring presence, and the sense of security Ox provides. These two could get on very well together as long as refined Rabbit can overlook Ox's occasional down-to-earth – Rabbit might say 'coarse' – observations.

Rabbit with Tiger

Surprisingly the Rabbit is not intimidated by Tiger's dangerous aura and this attitude immediately appeals to Tiger who enjoys a challenge. Rabbit's calm presence and clever way with words keeps Tiger interested, while Rabbit finds Tiger's adventurous tales entertaining. With care, these two could get on well together for years.

Rabbit Love 2020 Style

Wow! While the Year of the Rat is shaping up to be a pretty good year for you, Rabbit, the most fortunate area of your life is set to be your love life. This year you're so hot you could probably fry an egg on your outstretched paw, if it weren't such a vulgar suggestion.

Single Rabbits catch the eye wherever they go, and could even find themselves being fought over by more aggressive signs. You deplore such behaviour of course, Rabbit, but secretly, you're flattered.

Despite their wide eyes and innocent expression, Rabbits have a certain reputation where love is concerned, and this year the chances to play the field, or perhaps, play in the field, will arrive thick and fast. As long as it won't cause problems, unattached Rabbits can take advantage of their popularity.

Attached Rabbits can look forward to months of domestic bliss with their chosen one, as long as they resist the urge to give in to the mighty temptations outside the home.

This is particularly comforting when the Rat year's frantic pace gets wearying. Attached Rabbits can rely on hurrying home to their partner for all the joy and tranquillity they need. And don't be surprised if somewhere along the line this leads to an expansion of the Rabbit family. A baby bobtail will round off the year very nicely.

Secret of Success in 2020

You've got all the ingredients you need, Rabbit, to make 2020 a successful year. The only thing that could hamper you is your attitude.

You know that expression 'ratty'? As in, 'irritable', 'fault finding', 'snappy'? Strange that these negative moods are associated with the Rat because that's how Rat years can often make Rabbit feel.

The odd thing is that there's very little actually wrong to upset Rabbit. It's just something in the hectic atmosphere of these action-packed years that tends to make Rabbit tense, and 2020's metal element only adds to a sense of underlying stress.

Yet, in fact, the concern is mainly an illusion. It's just your mood Rabbit. Like a child that sees a dark shape under the bed and fears it's a monster, most of your worries will turn out to be nothing more than your imagination working overtime.

Trouble is, if you end up being unintentionally ratty with colleagues and friends who're only trying to help, you could lose a lot of valuable support.

Rabbits that get a grip, and realise their unease has little concrete cause, will sail on smoothly on over calm waters.

Maybe this is the year to take up yoga, meditation, or mindfulness, Rabbit, so you arrive serenely at the end of the year to claim your prize.

The Rabbit Year at a Glance

January – You arrive in 2020 on a roll from last year. Things are going well.

February – Watch out for coughs and colds. Cash comes in but goes out too.

March – A rival tries to sweet talk you. Don't fall for their games.

April – In Spring, Rabbits should take a break in the countryside.

May – A project is leading to success. Stick with it.

June – Exciting opportunities surround you. Pick at least one and go for it.

July – Colleagues look quarrelsome. Soothe misunderstandings.

August – Workmates still cranky. Persuade them to take a holiday or take one yourself.

September – Money's flowing in. Generosity will bring you good luck.

October – Someone has their eye on you and it could be love.

November – Envious types would like to steal something you own. Be careful. Lock up your valuables.

December – A lucky month. Time to celebrate an excellent year.

Lucky Colours 2019: Purple, Yellow, Green

Lucky Numbers 2019: 3, 4, 9

CHAPTER 6: THE DRAGON

龍

Dragon Years

23 January 1928 – 9 February 1929

8 February 1940 – 26 January 1941

27 January 1952 – 13 February 1953

13 February 1964 – 1 February 1965

31 January 1976 – 17 February 1977

17 February 1988 – 5 February 1989

5 February 2000 – 23 January 2001

23 January 2012 – 9 February 2013

10 February 2024 – 28 January 2025

Natural Element: Wood

Will 2020 be a Golden Year for the Dragon?

Should you feel a sudden urge to throw back your head and let out a glorious, joyous, blast of flame, Dragon, go right ahead! Because it looks like you'll be one of the luckiest signs of 2020.

You've been waiting a long time for your fortunes to change, Dragon, so go right ahead and enjoy the good news.

The last two years have been difficult for zodiac Dragons. 2018, ruled by the dour Dog, was particularly trying if you were typical of your sign, and while the Pig of 2019 was a lot more fun, most Dragons still got the sense of moving one step forward and two steps back.

The result has felt like an endless period of stagnation. Despite working very hard, many Dragons saw little in the way of reward or visible progress. Some fire breathers have felt tied down and trapped as a consequence; others suffered a big dent to their confidence.

Well, at long last, you've turned the corner. The reason is the industrious Rat and ebullient Dragon are great friends. Despite their disparity in size, they share the same dynamic energy and need to get things done. They work well together. In fact, this year many a Dragon and Rat will join forces in business, or Dragon could end up employing a key worker from the sign of the Rat, to their mutual advantage.

Water sign Rat will nurture Dragon's natural wood element and help Dragon projects grow and flourish. In turn, this year's metal element represents money, and helpful Rat will ensure it flows steadily into the Dragon bank account.

Once you've got used to the fact that your fortunes really have changed significantly for the better, Dragon, your confidence will soar and that wild imagination – dulled and limited for so long – can finally open its wings and fly.

Dragons are known for their originality. This quality of yours has been unappreciated these last couple of years, but now it comes into its own. Quirky ideas and schemes that seem a little off the wall will suddenly be in demand, and you could even end up becoming famous for them, Dragon.

Opportunities are suddenly all around. Many Dragons will change their jobs or accept a promotion – both options leading to an increase in pay. Other Dragons will be inspired to become self-employed or start a business. Possibly some particularly energetic Dragons will do all three.

Despite all this activity on the career front, a house move is entirely possible as well as a big upsurge in travel. It's as if the brakes have suddenly been released, or the prison door opened, and Dragon is off and eager to do absolutely everything at once.

This isn't a bad idea. With so much good luck on offer this year it makes sense to use it well and redesign the Dragon lifestyle so that it suits you beautifully for years to come.

There's likely to be a big expenditure near the beginning of the year, possibly home-related, but don't panic Dragon. You'll make so much money in the next 12 months the funds will be quickly replaced and then some.

All in all, 2020 could be the year you make your dreams come true.

What it means to be a Dragon in 2020

To be honest Dragon, it's not really fair. Your sign has so many advantages. When you're on good form, your personality is so dazzling the other signs need sunglasses.

The only mythical creature in the celestial cycle, in China the Dragon is associated with the Emperor and revered as a symbol of protection, power, and magnificence. No New Year celebration would be complete without the colourful Dragon, dancing through the streets, twisting and turning, and banishing evil spirits.

The Dragon is regarded as the most fortunate of signs and every couple hopes for a Dragon baby. A child born in a Dragon year is believed to bring good luck to the whole family and, to this day, the birth rate tends to rise about 5% in the Chinese community in Dragon years.

Dragons are usually strong, healthy, and blessed with enormous self-confidence and optimism. Even if they're not conventionally good-looking, they stand out in a crowd. They're charismatic with magnetic personalities, formidable energy, and people look up to them. Dragons are so accustomed to attention, they rarely question why this should be the case. It just seems like the natural way of the world.

These people think BIG. They're visionaries, bubbling with original new ideas, and their enthusiasm is so infectious, their optimism so strong, they easily inspire others. Without even trying, Dragons are born leaders and happily sweep their teams of followers into whatever new venture they've just dreamed up.

The only downside to this is that Dragons are easily bored. Trivial matters such as details irritate them, and they're keen to rush on to the next challenge before they've quite finished the first.

With a good second in command, who can attend to the picky minutiae, all could be well. If not, Dragon's schemes can go spectacularly wrong. Yet it hardly seems to matter. The Dragon ascribes to the theory that you have to fail your way to success. Setbacks are quickly forgotten as Dragon launches excitedly into the next adventure and quite often – given the Dragon's good luck – this works.

People born under this sign often receive success and wealth, yet they are not materialistic. They're generous and kind in an absent-minded way, and care far more about having a worthy goal than any rewards it might bring. And it is vital for the Dragon to have a goal. A Dragon without a goal is a sad, dispirited creature – restless and grumpy.

Even if it's not large, the Dragon home gives the impression of space and light. Dragons hate to feel confined in any way. They like to look out the window and see lots of sky and have clear, uncluttered surfaces around them, even if it's difficult for Dragons to keep them that way.

Yet the Dragon home could have a curiously un-lived-in feel. This is because the Dragon regards home as a lair – a comfortable base from which to plan the next project, rather than a place to spend a lot of time.

Dragons love to travel, but they don't really mind where they go as long as it's different and interesting. Yet, despite so much going for them, Dragons often feel misunderstood. Their impatience with trivia extends to the irritating need for tact and diplomacy at times. Dragon doesn't get this. If Dragon has something to say, they say it. Why waste time dressing it up in fancy words they think? But then people get upset, and Dragon is baffled. It's not always easy being a Dragon.

Best Jobs for Dragon

Journalist

Advertising

Company Director

TV Producer

Explorer

Judge

Inventor

Perfect Partners

Cupid's arrow can strike anywhere at any time, of course, but once the novelty of new romance wears off, some relationships are easier to maintain than others. Here's a guide to the Dragon's compatibility with other signs.

Dragon with Dragon

When Dragon meets Dragon, onlookers tend to take a step back and hold their breath. These two are a combustible mix – they either love each other or loathe each other. They are so alike it could go either way. Both dazzling in their own orbits, they can't fail to notice the other's charms but since they both need to be centre stage, things could get competitive. With give and take and understanding this match could work well, but it won't be easy.

Dragon with Snake

Surprisingly, this couple gets along beautifully. Snake's elegant appearance and quick but subtle mind intrigues Dragon, while Snake admires Dragon's success and endless energy. Snake has no need to battle for the limelight and is quite happy to sit back and support Dragon's schemes from the comfort of a stylish sofa. Which is all the encouragement Dragon needs.

Dragon with Horse

The athletic Horse is pretty good at keeping up with dashing Dragon. And Dragon appreciates a partner who enjoys getting out and about as much as Dragon does. Yet Horse might grow weary of Dragon's constant new projects and resent having to be involved. Horse likes to go off and do Horsey things at frequent intervals which Dragon tends to view as disloyal. This relationship could get fiery.

Dragon with Goat

Goat tends to baffle the busy Dragon. Dragon can see Goat is the creative type but can't understand why Goat doesn't appear to be working very hard when so much could be achieved. In fact, if they stayed together long enough, Dragon could help Goat make the most of many talents, but it's unlikely either of them can sustain enough interest for this to happen.

Dragon with Monkey

These two are likely to hit it off immediately. Each is attracted to the other's intelligence and lively presence, and Dragon's exuberance doesn't overwhelm hyperactive Monkey. What's more, though they both enjoy being surrounded by a crowd, Monkey only wants to make people laugh while Dragon hopes to inspire them to a cause. There is no conflict, so this couple can help each other to go far.

Dragon with Rooster

A Dragon and Rooster pairing will always attract attention. These two are both gorgeous beings and love to be surrounded by admirers. They will probably enjoy going out together and being seen as a couple, but in the long-term, they may not be able to provide the kind of support each secretly needs.

Entertaining for a while but probably not a lasting relationship.

Dragon with Dog

Not the easiest of combinations. Down-to-earth Dog can't see what all the fuss is about when it comes to Dragons. Unimpressed by glamour and irritated by what seems to Dog the gullibility of Dragon admirers, Dog can't be bothered to find out more. Dragon meanwhile is hurt by Dog's lack of interest. Great determination would be needed to make this work.

Dragon with Pig

While Dragon and Pig might seem to be opposites, the two of them can create a surprisingly contented relationship. Pig is quite happy for Dragon to fly around doing exciting things as long as Pig is not expected to do much more than admire profusely. Dragon appreciates Pig's uncritical support and makes allowances for Pig's lack of stamina. This couple could live in harmony.

Dragon with Rat

This couple is usually regarded as a very good match. They have much in common being action loving, excitement-seeking personalities who hate to be bored. It takes a lot to dazzle Rat, but the Dragon's glamorous aura proves irresistible, while Dragon loves to be admired, so each enjoys being with the other. There could be the odd power struggle as these two are both strong characters but the magnetism is so powerful they usually kiss and make up.

Dragon with Ox

Chalk and cheese though this pair may appear to be, there's a certain fascination between them. Ox may not approve of Dragon's showy manner but recognises Dragon's good intentions, while Dragon admires Ox's strength of character and gift for completing tasks. If each could find a way to tolerate the other's wildly different lifestyles, they might be good for each other but, long-term, Dragon's hectic pace might wear down even the Ox's legendary stamina.

Dragon with Tiger

The two biggest personalities in the zodiac would seem bound to clash. After all, these larger than life characters share so many similarities there's a danger they'd compete. Yet a relationship between the Tiger and Dragon often works well. They understand each other's impulsive natures, but they're also different enough to supply the support the other needs. They'd make a formidable power couple.

Dragon with Rabbit

Dragon is such a larger than life character, Rabbit could feel overwhelmed at times. Also, the Dragon can be rather noisy and over-dramatic which would get on Rabbit's nerves. Yet they each admire the other's good points. If they could live next door to each other instead of under the same roof, a long-term relationship might work.

Dragon Love 2020 Style

It will probably come as no surprise to hear that romance is not top of the single Dragon's to-do list this year.

As usual, all Dragons arouse interest wherever they go, and single Dragons won't be short of admirers; but, chances are, most of you will be having so much fun creating original adventures and planning intriguing trips, you won't notice a certain lack in the love department.

Single Dragons that would like to settle down could well find Mr or Ms Right in 2020, but after the past few years of playing it safe and staying home, chances are most will opt for a little light-hearted flirting, and steer clear of heavy involvement.

Attached Dragons will demand understanding from their partners. While, deep down, the Dragon wants security and affection and dislikes chopping and changing in relationships, this year more than ever they need to feel free.

Secrets of Success in 2020

Without going crazy, this is the year for thinking BIG, Dragon. This should come naturally to you, but after the previous few years – which have had a crushing effect – you might almost have forgotten how.

You've grown so accustomed to trimming things down, holding back, trying not to expect too much, that you've possibly become what passes for cautious in the Dragon brain.

It's time to rediscover your audacious, adventurous spirit. Don't jump off a cliff, of course, but – within reason – there's so much luck on your side, you can afford to take some calculated risks. This is the moment to think seriously about what you really want in life – and then go for it – no matter how ambitious.

That old saying 'shoot for the Moon because, even if you fail, you'll land among the stars,' could be your motto this year.

This is the moment to get your affairs back on the right track. Set things up now, in your lucky year, and the good fortune will carry you through the less fortunate times.

The only thing to watch out for, is your tendency to be a solo player. You'll do fine with your own efforts, Dragon, but even more brilliantly in a group in this sociable Rat year.

Also, take care that your returning confidence doesn't spill over into what other signs might see as arrogance. An overbearing Dragon will spark resentment – why alienate people when they could be your friends?

And, finally, remember that even indestructible Dragons need to work, rest, and play. Be certain to make time for all three.

The Dragon Year at a Glance

January – Things are getting better. You can feel it. A big expenditure looks likely. Don't worry. You can afford it.

February – Career projects are going well.

March – Past efforts look set to pay off big time. Don't spend it all before it arrives.

April – Spring puts even more bounce in your step. Get out and make the most.

May – Watch out for someone who is not quite what they seem. Double check all the details.

June – A sociable time. You're in demand, just don't tire yourself too much – there's still work to do.

July – You can afford to ease up a little, though you may not want to. Travel beckons.

August – Plenty of trips in the offing – not necessarily holidays. Combining business with pleasure suits you perfectly.

September – Summer adventures have given you something to think about. Use new ideas creatively.

October – Time to put in some more serious effort. A new venture looks exciting.

November – While others are slowing down, you're just getting your second wind. They can't understand how you do it.

December – It's party time and you've earned it. Invitations abound. Enjoy.

Lucky colours for 2020: Silver, Red

Lucky numbers for 2020: 1, 6, 7

CHAPTER 7: THE SNAKE

蛇

Snake Years

10 February 1929 – 29 January 1930

27 January 1941 – 14 February 1942

14 February 1953 – 2 February 1954

2 February 1965 – 20 January 1966

18 February 1977 – 6 February 1978

6 February 1989 – 26 January 1990

24 January 2001 – 11 February 2002

10 February 2013 – 30 January 2014

29 January 2025 – 16 February 2026

Natural Element: Fire

Will 2020 be a Golden Year for the Snake?

Intriguing – that's perhaps the best way to describe 2020 for the Snake. This is one of those years, Snake, when you're in the process of shedding your skin. That immensely clever trick you have of regenerating, of abandoning your old habits as if they were nothing to do with you, and walking away without a backward glance.

Last year, the year of the easy-going Pig, while not being ideal in every respect, gave many Snakes a chance to tread water, to maintain the balance of their lives while looking around, taking stock and deciding what direction they wanted to go in next.

If that sounds like you, Snake, the good news is that in 2020 you're likely to have a destination in mind, plus a handy map to guide you there.

It looks as if many Snakes will be inspired to begin to rebuild their lives to a whole new design this year, and – of course – being Snakes, they manage this transformation far better than any other sign.

There will be ups and downs, naturally, plus a little opposition from certain other signs who don't understand why you need to do what you need to do. But since Snake's attitude is often: 'Never complain, never explain,' you'll probably glide on in that unruffled, inscrutable way of yours, and do it anyway.

The reason for these bouts of friction is that the Rat belongs to the water element while the Snake is a fire creature. Fire likes to keep away from water wherever possible, and while there is an undeniable fascination from a distance between these two, if they get too close a lot of hissing and clouds of steam can ensue.

In day to day life, this is likely to cause weeks of progress interspersed with unexpected flare ups and criticism from colleagues or family.

Despite these minor spats, creative Snakes in particular will do very well under the Rat's beady eye. Highly detailed and beautifully decorative work will bring excellent rewards.

Earnings and windfalls will brighten the Snake life, as will careful investments. Property would be a good purchase for Snakes this year, too, as long as every aspect is thoroughly checked and investigated. The Rat's weakness for rushing things or falling for get-rich-quick schemes that turn out to be little more than wishful thinking can influence many signs in 2020 – don't be one of them Snake.

Employed Snakes could find their boss seems unfairly critical this year, but it may be because Snake's graceful yet languid way of going about things looks to the employer a lot like laziness. Rat energy just doesn't get the 'more haste, less speed' theory at all, while Snake is a life-long devotee.

If you have to put up with such an unsympathetic person in your life, Snake, the best plan is to pal up with a Dragon or Monkey friend or colleague. They'll know exactly how to handle them and turn things around for you.

Self-employed Snakes, with only themselves to please, on the other hand, can look forward to a steady stream of new opportunities and fresh faces coming into their orbit.

Yet, delightful as this is, many Snakes will be more interested in their life-changing, restructuring process this year. If this is you, you'll be relishing a new-found freedom and once you've got it, you'll be very reluctant to let it go.

Some Snakes will find themselves drawn towards spiritual interests and healing, others creative work and the arts, but whichever direction you choose, Snake, you're laying down foundations in 2020 that could influence your future for years to come.

What it Means to Be a Snake in 2020

Imagine for a moment a creature that was incredibly beautiful, wise, intelligent, graceful, sophisticated and respected. A creature always unhurried, yet attaining its goals, apparently without effort.

What would you call this amazing beast? Well if you were Chinese you'd probably call it a Snake. That's right – a Snake.

Here, in the West, Snakes are almost as unwelcome as Rats and have been ever since Eve was persuaded to eat that apple in the Garden of Eden by a wily serpent. Most of us wouldn't have a good word to say for Snakes. Yet, in the East, it's a different story. There, all manner of positive qualities are discerned in the Snake, and the zodiac Snake is a good sign to be born under.

What's more, if we can forget all preconceived notions and look afresh at the much-maligned serpent, we have to admit there's something quite remarkable – almost magical – about the Snake.

For a start, Snakes don't have eyelids, which makes their stare particularly disconcerting. Astonishingly, they can shed their entire skins without ill effect, and slide away with a brand new, rejuvenated, wrinkle-free body – a feat many a human would envy.

Then there's the way they slither along without the need for legs – a bit repellent to a lot of people, but it can't be denied there's something uncanny about it. It's a surprisingly efficient means of locomotion too, and at times Snakes can move with astonishing speed. Quite a few of them can do this in water as well as on land which makes them remarkably adaptable.

Snakes are in no way cuddly, but it seems even in the West we've retained a faint memory of a time when we recognised wisdom in the serpent. The Rod of Asclepius – the familiar symbol of a snake twisted around a pole – is still a widely used and recognised medical sign, seen outside pharmacies and doctors' surgeries, even if we don't know that Asclepius was the Greek God associated with healing. And in Greece, in the dim and distant past, snakes were sacred and believed to aid the sick.

The Chinese zodiac Snake is regarded as possibly the most beautiful of all the creatures, and people born under this sign somehow manage to present themselves in such an artful way, they give the illusion of beauty, even if not naturally endowed.

The Snake is physically graceful too. Each movement flowing into the next with effortless, elegant economy. Even when they're in a hurry, Snakes appear calm and unrushed, and should they arrive late for an appointment they're so charming and plausible with their excuses they're always forgiven.

This is a sign of great intelligence and subtlety. Snakes are never pushy, yet can usually slide into the heart of any situation they choose. Their clever conversation and easy charm makes them popular at any gathering. Yet, the Snake is picky. Snakes prefer to conserve their energy and don't waste it on activities and people of no interest to them. They are self-contained, quite happy with their own company if necessary, and seldom bored.

At work, Snakes are quietly ambitious, but in line with their policy of conserving energy wherever possible, they will aim for the quickest, easiest route to their goals. Just as the mythical Snake crossed the celestial river wrapped around the hoof of the Horse, the Snake is quite content to link their fortunes to those of a rising star so that Snake is carried to the top in their wake. Ever practical, the Snake has no need for an ego massage – the end result is what matters.

Other signs often mistake Snake's economy of action for laziness, but this is short-sighted. In fact, the Snake is so efficient and so clever that tasks are completed with great speed, leaving Snake with plenty of time to relax afterwards. What's more, in the same way that a Snake can shed its skin, people born under this sign are quite capable of suddenly walking out of a situation or way of life that no longer suits them, and reinventing themselves elsewhere without regret.

They tend to do this without warning, leaving their previous companions stunned. Only afterwards do people learn that the Snake has been inert and silently brooding for months. But it's no good imploring Snake to return. Snake's actions are swift and irrevocable.

The Snake home is a lovely place. Snakes have perfect taste. They like art, design, good lighting, and comfort. They're excellent hosts. They may not entertain often, unless they can delegate the chores, but when they do, they make it a stylish occasion to remember.

Snakes are known for their love of basking in the sun, and zodiac Snakes are no exception. Trips involving long hikes uphill in the pouring rain will not impress the Snake, but a smart sun-lounger by an infinity pool in a tropical paradise… well, that would be Snake's idea of heaven.

Best Jobs for Snake

Councillor

Psychiatrist

Doctor

Holistic Therapist

Teacher

Adviser

Psychic Medium

Perfect Partners

Cupid's arrow can strike anywhere at any time, of course, but once the novelty of new romance wears off, some relationships are easier to maintain than others. Here's a guide to the Snake's compatibility with other signs.

Snake with Snake

This fine looking couple turn heads wherever they go. Beautiful and perfectly dressed these two look like the perfect match. They never stop talking and enjoy the same interests so this could be a successful relationship. Long-term, however, there could be friction. They're both experts at getting what they want using the same sophisticated techniques, so they can see through each other.

Snake with Horse

At some level, perhaps, Horse remembers how Snake beat him in the calendar race, so despite an initial attraction, these two could be wary of each other. Snake is impressed by Horse's energy and athleticism while Horse admires Snake's elegance and charm. Yet they don't really have much in common. Deep thinking Snake could find Horse rather shallow and Horse may see Snake as frustratingly enigmatic.

Snake with Goat

Snake and Goat could enjoy many happy hours touring art galleries and exhibitions together. Neither of them craves excitement and harsh, adrenalin-boosting activities, and both appreciate creative artistic personalities. There's no pressure to compete with each other so these two would sail along quite contentedly. Not a passionate alliance but they could be happy.

Snake with Monkey

These two clever creatures ought to admire each other if only for their fine minds and, at first, it's possible they might. But unless they're really determined to make it work, it won't be long before active Monkey finds Snake's energy-saving ways irritating, while Snake loses patience with Monkey's endless jokes.

Snake with Rooster

Surprisingly, Snake and Rooster work well together. Both gorgeous in different ways, they complement each other without competing. Snake's keen eyes can see beneath Rooster's proud facade to the sensitive, unsure person inside, while Rooster appreciates Snake's unobtrusive strength and wise words of encouragement at just the right moment. These two could be inseparable.

Snake with Dog

Some snakes seem to have an almost hypnotic power and, for some reason, Dog is particularly susceptible to these skills. We've heard of snake-charmers but snakes can be dog-charmers and without even trying, Snakes can find themselves the recipients of Dog devotion. Since the Dog is strong, loyal, and can be fun, Snake is not averse to this but might, in the end, find it boring.

Snake with Pig

Pig and Snake don't have a lot to say to each other. Snake can't be bothered with Pig's endless shopping, and Pig is hurt by Snake's snobbish attitude. They both enjoy the good things in life so a luxury fling could briefly be fun – a shared spa break might be a good idea – but in the long-term, this relationship is probably not worth pursuing.

Snake with Rat

The Snake shares Rat's good taste and being elegant, sophisticated, and smart will delight Rat at first sight. These two get on very well on an intellectual level but perhaps are better as good friends rather than long-term partners. The Snake's love of basking in the sun for hours strikes Rat as lazy and dull, while Rat's need to rush around doing deals and meeting people seems pointless and wearying to Snake.

Snake with Ox

Like Ox, the Snake is quietly ambitious and not given to racing around unless it's absolutely necessary. Ox, on the other hand, respects Snake's clever brain and understated elegance. These two could quickly discover how beneficial an alliance between them would be. They're both happy to give the other space when required but also step in with support when needed. This could be a very successful match.

Snake with Tiger

Not the best of romances. These two are so fundamentally different that any initial attraction is unlikely to last. Snake likes to bask and soak up the sun while Tiger wants to explore and discover. Tiger takes in the big picture at a glance and is off to the next challenge while Snake likes to pause, delve beneath the surface, and consider matters. It wouldn't take long before these two annoy each other.

Snake with Rabbit

This subtle pair could make a good combination. They both understand the value of working behind the scenes and neither has any desire to wear themselves out on endless adventures. They share a love of art, fine things, and quiet pleasures and they both enjoy an orderly home. These two could settle down very happily together.

Snake with Dragon

Surprisingly, this couple gets along beautifully. Snake's elegant appearance and quick but subtle mind intrigues Dragon, while Snake admires Dragon's success and endless energy. Snake has no need to battle for the limelight and is quite happy to sit back and support Dragon's schemes from the comfort of a stylish sofa. Which is all the encouragement Dragon needs.

Snake Love 2020 Style

Sensuous Snakes are very much in demand this year. The Rat finds Snake entrancing, if puzzling, and single Snakes are likely to be inundated with tempting invitations in the next few months.

You'll probably be happy enough to go with the flow and experiment with different personalities, Snake, but it's unlikely you'll want to commit yourself for the long-term. Deep down, you're planning that new future and you haven't made up your mind yet as to the type of partner you'd like to share it with.

Whether you're single or attached, you could find you have to deal with an admirer who won't take no for an answer. This person has become obsessed with you – a situation that happens with Snakes from time to time – and you'll have to discourage them in your usual tactful way. This won't be easy but as a Snake, chances are you've dealt with it before so you know how to handle it.

Settled Snakes have a choice. You can carry on in the same way with your partner if you're content or you can consider where they fit into your plan for the future. If the answer seems to be 'they don't', this is probably the year you'll start disengaging. On the other hand, maybe it's worth sounding them out about rebuilding a future together. You never know. Their response may surprise you.

Secrets of Success in 2020

It's quite likely you're thinking long-term this year, Snake, so you're not expecting, or even wanting, to reach all your goals in the next 12 months. That would imply those goals were fairly small and easily attained while you're thinking BIG! You understand well that major, life-enhancing changes take time to come to fruition.

Success for Snakes in 2020, therefore, involves laying a number of carefully thought-out plans, taking the necessary steps to get them up and running, and then standing back to watch them grow.

As a Snake, you have all the patience you need to benefit from this strategy and you've never been the type to see the point in expending unnecessary energy. Yet, even the most far-sighted Snake can't live in the future. You've got to make the most of the here and now, too. That's where it will be an excellent policy to ally yourself with friends and colleagues who're best friends with the Rat – Dragons and Monkeys in particular – and join forces with them. Together, you can move mountains.

Always remember that – ludicrous as it seems to a clever mind like yours – the Rat demands you appear to be busy and working hard at all times. You know, of course, that it's results that count, but if you can humour the Rat, and at least look as if you're pouring your heart and soul into the task at hand, you'll do well.

Finally, always take care to pace yourself. The Rat's frenetic scurrying can wear out languorous Snakes. Get out and bask in warm sunshine as often as you can.

The Snake Year at a Glance

January – Normally discreet, you want to have your say this month. Be careful hasty words don't get you into trouble.

February – Cash comes and goes. A nice increase could slip through your fingers. Stay alert.

March – A blast from the past could take you by surprise. If you're pleased to see them, this could be interesting.

April – Golden opportunities are showering around you. Grab them and watch them grow.

May – Things are looking good but don't ease up yet. More effort will pay off.

June – A new person has entered your circle but they may not be what they seem. Don't give your trust too soon.

July – You've already come a long way this year. Those beneficial changes are beginning to show.

August – It's the holiday season and vacationing Snakes enjoy a new romance.

September – Carefully laid plans are coming to fruition. Don't celebrate too soon. Discipline and patience will carry you through.

October – Irritating people cross your path. Don't let them upset you. Smile but keep your distance.

November – Sexy stars are shining. A whirlwind romance could take your breath away.

December – You're in the mood to party, and you're buying lots of gifts. Watch out for envious eyes, but enjoy the season.

Lucky colours 2020: Purple, black, Green

Lucky Numbers 2020: 3, 7, 8

CHAPTER 8: THE HORSE

馬

Horse Years

30 January 1930 – 16 February 1931

15 February 1942 – 4 February 1943

3 February 1954 – 23 January 1955

21 January 1966 – 8 February 1967

7 February 1978 – 27 January 1979

27 January 1990 – 14 February 1991

12 February 2002 – 31 January 2003

31 January 2014 – 18 February 2015

17 February 2026 – 5 February 2027

Natural Element: Fire

Will 2020 be a Golden Year for the Horse?

Beautiful, headstrong Horse will have to canter carefully to make the most of this year.

Whereas last year – ruled by the cosy, contented Pig – started well for the Horse but then gradually may have seemed a little dull, the Rat brings a powerful new energy which might arrive as a shock to the system after the comparatively tranquil months before.

If you're typical of your sign, you're all for action and activity. Horses love to be out and about, making things happen, so in theory the increase in tempo should be welcome.

Yet the trouble is, the zodiac Rat and the zodiac Horse don't get along too well together. The Rat belongs to the water element whereas the Horse is a fire creature. From a distance, the Rat can't help but admire the glorious Horse but in character, deep down, these two are opposites who don't really understand each other.

What's more, traditionally, the fire element is believed to be afraid of water for obvious reasons, so prefers to keep well away, to prevent being doused.

In day-to-day life, this could manifest as a series of misunderstandings arising where least expected, and a string of critical, annoying people crossing Horse's path.

This is not the best time to consider changing jobs unless you really have to, Horse, because it will be more difficult to present your finest qualities to their best advantage.

On the other hand, Horses already in employment could do exceptionally well with the right attitude. This is because, this year, no matter what their actual birth sign, Horse employers are represented by the Rat and Rat energy. So, the Horse is making money for the Rat, which the Rat appreciates greatly.

As long as the Horse demonstrates loyalty, discipline, and a good work ethic, the Rat will ensure well-earned rewards flow generously.

What's more, there's a good chance this year that Horses will impress the boss by creating a new, more efficient way of completing a task or streamlining an existing system in an original way. Your ingenuity won't go unnoticed, and will do wonders for your future prospects.

Social stars look bright too. Both the Horse and the Rat love being surrounded by friends, so this year you'll do well in any area that involves being part of a group.

Invitations to parties, get-togethers, and sporting events will pour your way and you'll enjoy yourself. Just take care not to get dragged into arguments with those irritating types that seem drawn to you like wasps to a picnic this year.

Do that Horse thing of tossing your mane, and trotting away with dignity.

Financially, many Horses could be in for a pleasant surprise. Unexpected windfalls and cash boosts could come your way when you least expect it. There's a danger, though, that you might be tempted to treat yourself to some extravagant goodies.

This is understandable. You've earned a treat or two, after all. Nevertheless, Horses that budget carefully, and stash away as much as they can afford, will be amazed how their wealth can accumulate.

All in all, despite 2020 not being the easiest of years for the Horse, Horses can do very well if they keep calm, control their tempers, and be ready to respond to opportunities in an instant.

What it means to be a Horse in 2020

Sleek and graceful, as well as strong and swift, the Horse has always been an object of admiration and often longing. Young girls dream of having their own pony while many adults, on acquiring a pile of cash, often treat themselves to a race horse or at least a share in one.

In China, the Horse is believed to be a symbol of freedom and you've only got to see a picture of the famous white horses of the Camargue, exuberantly splashing through the marshes, to understand why.

People born in the year of the Horse exude a similar magnificence. They tend to be strong and athletic with broad shoulders and fine heads of thick hair. Where would the Horse be without its mane? Most Horses excel at sports, especially when young. They can run fast if they choose, but they will happily try any game until they find the one that suits them best.

Horses, being herd animals, are gregarious types and don't like to spend too long alone. They enjoying hanging out with a crowd, chatting and swapping gossip, and Horses of both sexes can lap up any amount of grooming. They love having their hair brushed and fussed over, their nails manicured; a facial or relaxing massage is usually welcome.

Yet, Horses are more complex than they first appear. The affable, easy-going charmer, delighting everyone at a party, can suddenly take offence at a casual remark or storm off in a huff over some tiny hitch almost unnoticeable to anyone else, leaving companions baffled. They tend to stay baffled too, because it's difficult to get a handle on what upsets the Horse since what annoys them one week may leave them completely unruffled the next.

The trouble is, although they look tough, Horses are in fact very sensitive. Inside, they're still half wild. Their senses are incredibly sharp, and although they don't realise it, deep down they're constantly scanning the horizon and sniffing the air for the first signs of danger. As a result, Horses live on their nerves. They tend to over-react when things don't go completely to plan, and have to work hard to control a sense of panic.

Ideally, Horses would like to bolt away when the going gets rough but as this is not usually possible, they get moody and difficult instead.

Provide calm, congenial conditions for a Horse, however, and you couldn't wish for a friendlier companion. The Horse is lively, enthusiastic, versatile, and fun.

At work, the Horse wants to do well but can't stand being fenced in or forced to perform repetitive, routine tasks. Also, although they're good in a team, Horses have a need for privacy and independence so they may change jobs frequently until they find the right role. Yet, when they're happy, Horses will shine.

At home, Horse is probably planning the next trip. Horses like to be comfortable but they're not the most domesticated of the signs. They love being in the open air and don't see the point of spending too much time wallowing on a sofa or polishing dusty ornaments. They may well spend more time in the garden than indoors. On holiday, Horse loves to head for wide open spaces – a vast beach, a craggy hillside or a mountain meadow; Horse would be thrilled to explore them all.

Best Jobs for Horse

Travelling Salesman

Sportsman

Jockey

Hairdresser

Estate Agent

Dog Groomer

Driving Instructor

Party Planner

Perfect Partners

Cupid's arrow can strike anywhere at any time, of course, but once the novelty of new romance wears off, some relationships are easier to maintain than others. Here's a guide to the Horse's compatibility with other signs.

Horse with Horse

No doubt about it, these two make a magnificent couple, and any foals in the family would be spectacular. They certainly understand each other, particularly their shared need for both company and alone time so, in general, they get on well. The only tricky part could come if they both grew anxious over the same issue at the same time. Neither would find it easy to calm the other.

Horse with Goat

Goat and Horse just click! These two love kicking up their heels and trotting off into the green. Goat doesn't need to go far or do anything strenuous but is always up for a break in routine, while Horse doesn't do routine at all so is constantly on the lookout for a partner ready to escape. This couple rarely considers the consequences but, mostly, they don't need to.

Horse with Monkey

Uh oh – best not attempted unless it's love at first sight. Monkey and Horse have wildly different outlooks and can't seem to see eye to eye on anything. They're both lively but in different ways that don't complement each other. Monkey will consider Horse's moods illogical and pointless while Horse is irritated that Monkey makes no attempt to understand how Horse feels. Very hard work.

Horse with Rooster

The eye-catching Rooster intrigues Horse while Rooster appreciates Horse's strength and agility. They can enjoy many stimulating dates together. Yet, in the long-run, this couple may not be able to provide the stability the other needs. They're both sensitive types but in different ways. After a while, the relationship could run out of steam.

Horse with Dog

Both good friends of man, these two can make a formidable team. Dog understands the occasional need for solitude while admiring Horse's strength and agility. Horse, meanwhile, senses Dog's loyalty and down to earth nature. Both lovers of the great outdoors and physical activity, they'll never be short of adventures to share. A promising long-term relationship.

Horse with Pig

Pig and Horse are good companions. Horse is soothed by easy-going Pig and Pig is proud to be seen with such an alluring creature as Horse. They don't have a lot of interests in common but they don't antagonise each other either. They can jog along amicably for quite a while but long-term they may find they each want more than the other can provide.

Horse with Rat

Rat and Horse both fizz with energy and they love action and looking good, yet this is not seen as an ideal partnership. Nothing's impossible of course but these two will have to work hard to find harmony. The Rat will admire Horse's enthusiasm and cheerful approach but become impatient to discover Horse can also be fiery and emotional. Horse, on the other hand, can find Rat's risk-taking behaviour extremely worrying.

Horse with Ox

Long ago on many Western farms, Ox was replaced by the Horse, and it may be that Ox has never forgotten and never forgiven. At any rate, these two, despite both being big, strong animals are not usually friends. Horse is too flighty and frivolous to interest Ox for long, while Ox's methodical, careful ways will irritate the Horse. Best not to go there.

Horse with Tiger

This athletic pair gets on pretty well. They both like physical pursuits, testing their strength out of doors or just enjoying the feel of the wind in their hair and the ground under their feet. True, Horse may not quite understand Tiger's plans for world domination but it doesn't really matter. Horse is happy to be loyal to such a charismatic partner. As they're both moody, there could be rows but making up is exciting.

Horse with Rabbit

This could be tricky. It's fairly unlikely that Horse and Rabbit would ever end up on a date but if they did and there was a strong attraction, it could lead to a love/hate relationship. Rabbit's neat and tidy ways would enrage Horse and Horse's unpredictable moods and over-the-top reactions would annoy Rabbit. Soon, Horse is likely to bolt for the hills or Rabbit retreat to its burrow.

Horse with Dragon

The athletic Horse is pretty good at keeping up with dashing Dragon. And Dragon appreciates a partner who enjoys getting out and about as much as Dragon does. Yet Horse might grow weary of Dragon's constant new projects and resent having to be involved. Horse likes to go off and do Horsey things at frequent intervals which Dragon tends to view as disloyal. This relationship could get fiery.

Horse with Snake

At some level, perhaps Horse remembers how Snake beat him in the calendar race, so despite an initial attraction, these two could be wary of each other. Snake is impressed by Horse's energy and athleticism while Horse admires Snake's elegance and charm. Yet they don't really have much in common. Deep thinking Snake could find Horse rather shallow and Horse may see Snake as frustratingly enigmatic.

Horse Love 2020 Style

Single Horses never lack for attention. With your striking good looks, glossy hair, and beautiful eyes, you tend to get noticed wherever you go. This year, favouring as it does group activities and socialising, is the perfect setting for gregarious Horses to make a big impression.

You'll find your diary full of exciting events and you're just going to love dashing from one to another. Chances are, when you leave, you'll be trailing a new conquest in your wake.

Whether you find your soulmate along the way, though, is debateable. It's not impossible. It's just that 2020's habit of throwing misunderstandings in Horse's path could mean the route to true love is more fiery than usual. Single Horses could find themselves on a passionate roller coaster – madly in love one moment, quarrelling the next.

Yet, since Horse is quite capable of galloping away at the first sign of trouble – before things have become too serious – single Horses will probably revel in the variety.

Spoken-for Horses could enjoy a wonderful 12 months with their partners as long as they try to avoid silly arguments. Bear in mind that your other half's not being deliberately critical – it's probably that you can be a bit moody at times, Horse, and this year's energy makes you super-sensitive.

Secret of Success in 2020

Success can be yours in 2020, Horse, but you'll have to work smarter for it than last year. The cleverest thing you can do is keep cool and resolve not to take things personally.

Chances are that annoying circumstances you meet may be irritating, but they're not necessarily about you. Horses that resist the impulse to fly into a sulk or stalk off, and calmly hang around to discuss the situation with tact, will quickly find a solution.

This diplomatic approach combined with genuine hard graft will work wonders, Horse. You could see yourself powering up the career ladder with astonishing speed, and your success will be reflected in your swelling bank balance.

Above all, the canny Horse will strenuously avoid any suggestion to bend the rules or sail close to the wind with legal matters. Other signs might get away with taking such chances this year, Horse, but you won't.

Make sure everything you do is a shining example of your finest equine integrity, and you can't go wrong.

Finally – the bit you're best at – get ready to release your inner race-horse. Fabulous opportunities will be speeding by at lightning pace this year, Horse, and only the fastest will catch them.

The Horse Year at a Glance

January – You're ready for a new challenge. Fresh options are stirring.

February – An unexpected windfall comes your way. Helpful friends arrive.

March – An unusual idea could prove profitable. Investigate further.

April – The boss is taking an interest in you right now, but a colleague could get jealous.

May – Quarrelsome folk prove annoying. Stay out of arguments.

June – Career gets a boost. Your efforts are recognised. Keep doing what you're doing.

July – Cash is rolling in. Don't go mad but treat yourself – you deserve it.

August – After all that effort, you could do with a break. The perfect time to take a holiday.

September – Reunions and get-togethers beckon. Revamp your look.

October – Property matters come to the fore. If you fancy a change of scene, look around but make no hasty moves.

November – Socialising steps up a notch. Work's still busy but make time to party.

December – You're glad to wind down, but happy to count all the cash you've made this year.

Lucky Colours for 2020: Brown, yellow, purple

Lucky Numbers for 2020: 2, 3, 7

CHAPTER 9: THE GOAT

羊

Goat Years

17 February 1931 – 5 February 1932

5 February 1943 – 24 January 1944

24 January 1955 – 11 February 1956

9 February 1967 – 29 January 1968

28 January 1979 – 15 February 1980

15 February 1991 – 3 February 1992

1 February 2003 – 21 January 2004

19 February 2015 – 7 February 2016

6 February 2027 – 25 January 2028

Natural Element: Fire

Will 2020 be a Golden Year for the Goat?

Charming, happy-go-lucky Goats prefer their years to come smooth and light-hearted, with not too many surprises. Well, so do other signs, of course, but Goats more than most.

For this reason, while Goats have a lot to look forward to in 2020, many could find the unexpected, spontaneous events that will bubble up from time to time a shade uncomfortable, even though they're beneficial.

The Rat has nothing against Goats. In fact, the Rat finds Goat rather delightful, so the energy this year is not hostile to cloven-footed creatures. And the Goat, for Goat's part, is perfectly happy in Rat's company. So, in theory, all should be well.

The only trouble is that these two signs have fundamentally different ways of going about their business. Rat's fast-paced, often daring manoeuvres tend to make Goat nervous because despite that relaxed, laid-back exterior, Goat is a secret worrier. Rat, on the other hand, finds Goat's apparent lack of 'drive' puzzling, and itches to give his furry friend a helpful kick up the backside. Which, of course, is not helpful at all as far as Goat is concerned.

Then there's the matter of their opposing elements. As the Rat is a water sign and the Goat a fire creature, the opposite elements can manifest in day to day life as friction and irritations. If you're typical of your sign, you may find you encounter far more argumentative people than usual this year, Goat, and since you're a sensitive soul who loathes quarrels, this could be upsetting.

Yet the outlook, particularly for your career, is excellent. Goats in fields where commission is paid will do exceptionally well, and artistic Goats or Goats with an unusual talent could achieve results that are spectacular. Fame and fortune could be in store for these fortunate creatures.

Many Goats will be offered promotion this year or lured away to a new job. Financially, this will make good sense, but think carefully all the same. New roles in a Rat year come with demands that gentle Goat can find uncomfortably pressured. If it looks too stressful, it might be better to say 'no'.

Whatever you decide, Goat, it looks like more money will work its way to you somehow. You may even find yourself in line for an inheritance or a win of some kind. This is ideal because there's nothing Goats like better than being financially free to pursue the far more interesting aspects of life.

There will be many chances to spend though, particularly on highly entertaining social events. You're going to adore it, Goat, but be careful not to end up being too extravagant and blowing the lot.

And much as you crave tranquillity and a stable environment, you could find yourself moving home this year, Goat. In fact, despite your instinct to dig your heels in and resist change, by the time the year of the Rat has passed, chances are your life will be looking quite different from the way it looks today. And you're going to love it.

What it Means to be a Goat in 2020

If people born under the sign of the Goat tend to look a little puzzled, uncertain even, who could blame them? It's not even definite their sign is the Goat. Some authorities call their sign the Sheep. Others – the more macho types – have it down as the Ram.

The confusion seems to stem from different translations of the original Chinese word.

But what's in a name? Whatever you call it, the qualities ascribed to the Goat/Sheep/Ram are the same. In China, the sign is regarded as symbolising peace and harmony. What's more, it's the eighth sign of the zodiac and the number eight is believed to be a very lucky number, associated as it is with growth and prosperity.

So, all you confused Goats out there can relax in the knowledge you were born in a lucky year.

In truth, perhaps the gentle sheep – the living animal that is – does resemble the zodiac Goat more than the real-life goat. Flesh and blood goats tend to have a feisty, combative quality and a strongly stubborn streak. Those sharp, pointy horns and all that head-butting does tend to put people off.

Yet, people born in a Goat year are known as the sweetest and friendliest of all the signs. They possess no spikey quality at all. They are tolerant and kind, have no wish to be competitive, and want to see the best in everyone they meet. Though they may not realise it, this attitude often unconsciously brings out the best in others, so the Goat's expectations are usually fulfilled.

Goats seem to get on with almost everyone, even people that others can't abide.

What's more Goats usually possess a wonderful artistic talent. Even those Goats who feel they can't paint, draw, or manage anything skilled, are nevertheless immensely creative with a fine eye for colour and design.

The Goat loves beautiful things and even sees beauty in objects and places that hold no appeal for others. They love to use their hands in their spare time, ideally making something practical yet decorative. Knitting, card-making, cake-decorating, gardening, or renovating old furniture, even DIY, will give them great pleasure.

Concepts such as time and also money, have little meaning for the Goat. When the Goat gets lost in inspiration, hours pass in seconds and Goat ends up late for anything else that might have been on the agenda.

Similarly, money is frustrating for the Goat. Goats are not materialistic, neither are they particularly ambitious in a worldly way. Objects other people regard as status symbols hold little Goat appeal so they can't see the point of putting in a lot of energy to acquire them. For this reason, Goats are not career-driven. All they really want to do is pursue their artistic project or latest interest. If this won't provide an income though, they'll do their best at whatever job turns up, in order to get back to their true vocation at weekends.

The perfect scenario for the Goat would be a big win on the lottery so they never have to waste time on a conventional job again. Should this ever happen, they'd be advised to get someone else to look after the funds for them; Goats are not good at handling finances and the windfall could slip through their fingers with distressing speed.

Goats are notoriously impractical with matters such as bills, household repairs, filling in forms, and meeting deadlines. They just can't seem to find the time to tackle such mundane items. Though they're intelligent people, they'll frequently claim not to understand such things. The truth is, of course, the ultra-creative Goat brain just can't be bothered.

One thing Goats do have in common with the flesh and blood animal is their stubborn streak. Despite that easy-going, sunny nature, zodiac Goats can astonish their friends by suddenly digging in their heels over what looks to others like a trivial matter of very little importance. Once Goat has adopted this position, it will not budge, no matter how unreasonable or how poor the outcome is likely to be.

The Goat home is an intriguing place. Striking and original, it's likely to be filled with mismatched treasures Goat has picked up along the way. Goats love car boot sales, junk shops, and galleries. They enjoy beach-combing and collecting branches and broken wood on country walks. They've even been known to 'rescue' items from rubbish skips. Somehow, Goat manages to weave together the most unpromising items to create a pleasing effect.

Best Jobs for Goat in 2020

Painter

Ceramic Workshop Worker

Musician

Cosmetic or Car Sales

Garden Designer

Colour Therapist

Antiques Restorer

Perfect Partners

Cupid's arrow can strike anywhere at any time, of course, but once the novelty of new romance wears off, some relationships are easier to maintain than others. Here's a guide to the Goat's compatibility with other signs.

Goat with Goat

When things are going well, you won't find a happier couple than two Goats. They are perfectly in tune with each other's creative natures and understand when to do things together and when to step back and give the other space. And since they both share the same interests, their together times are always fun. Yet, when practical problems arise, neither can easily cope. With a helpful friend on speed-dial, this would work.

Goat with Monkey

Monkey and Goat are different but in a good way. Though they don't quite 'get' each other deep down, Goat admires Monkey's lively personality and magical ability to come up with solutions for everything, while curious Monkey enjoys Goat's knowledge of the arts and the unusual. Long-term, Goat might not present enough of a challenge for Monkey but, with effort, it's a promising match.

Goat with Rooster

Peaceful Goat is not one to make feathers fly so these two are unlikely to fall out, but they're unlikely to find perfect compatibility either. Goat is unable to give Rooster the regular ego boosts that make Rooster thrive while Rooster is baffled by Goat's unpredictable devotion to impractical projects or people. Misunderstandings are likely.

Goat with Dog

This is another relationship that could be tricky. Loyal Dog would be quite willing to stand by Goat when practical problems loom but could end up irritated by Goat's inability to learn from previous mistakes and so keeps making them. Goat can't understand why Dog gets so bothered. With care, these two could learn to live together.

Goat with Pig

Happy-go-lucky Pig and laid-back Goat make a good pair. They hate to stir up trouble and always look for a peaceful solution to any challenge. Ideally, they'd avoid the challenge altogether. They could be very contented together as long as Pig's spending and Goat's inability to deal with finances doesn't get them into trouble.

Goat with Rat

The Rat is charmed by carefree Goat and fascinated by its artistic talent and happy knack of living in the present. Easy-going Goat tends to like everyone so is perfectly content to enjoy Rat's company. These two can get along fine, yet they don't really understand each other deep down. Long-term, the Rat may find Goat's lack of interest in the practical side of life irritating.

Goat with Ox

Though these two share artistic natures (even if in the case of the Ox, they're well hidden), deep down they don't 'get' one another. Ox may be beguiled at first by Goat's friendly, easy-going manner but then disappointed to discover Goat seems to find everyone equally delightful, even those who are plainly unworthy. Goat, on the other hand, can't understand why Ox won't lighten up more. This relationship would require a lot of effort and compromise.

Goat with Tiger

Tiger and Goat don't have a lot in common. While their aims and temperaments are quite different, they are both sociable creatures and Goat wouldn't mind Tiger attracting all the attention when they're out together. Tiger in return would appreciate Goat's lack of jealousy and generosity of spirit. Yet, long-term, they're likely to drift apart as they follow their different interests.

Goat with Dragon

Goat tends to baffle the busy Dragon. Dragon can see Goat is the creative type but can't understand why Goat doesn't appear to be working very hard when so much could be achieved. In fact, if they stayed together long enough, Dragon could help Goat make the most of many talents but it's unlikely either of them can sustain enough interest for this to happen.

Goat with Snake

Snake and Goat could enjoy many happy hours touring art galleries and exhibitions together. Neither of them craves excitement and harsh, adrenalin-boosting activities and both appreciate creative, artistic personalities. There's no pressure to compete with each other so these two would sail along quite contentedly. Not a passionate alliance but they could be happy.

Goat with Horse

Goat and Horse just click! These two love kicking up their heels and trotting off into the green. Goat doesn't need to go far or do anything strenuous but is always up for a break in routine, while Horse doesn't do routine at all so is constantly on the lookout for a partner ready to escape. This couple rarely considers the consequences, but mostly, they don't need to.

Goat Love 2020 Style

Spontaneity is the name of the game this year, Goat, and when it comes to love that's fine with you. This is a party year for Goats and you'll sail out, dressed in your normal, original-yet-quirky style which can't help but catch the eye. It won't be long before you're surrounded by other signs, eager to get to know you and perhaps tempt you on to other revelries later.

This is where spontaneity comes in. Don't do anything risky, but unexpected encounters and unusual invitations could lead to love for single Goats. Don't reject the unfamiliar out of habit and accept those last minute, out of the blue dates. You never know where they might lead.

Once again, that tricky fire and water mix looks likely to bring you into the orbit of some difficult characters who're spoiling for a row, but as your sign is peace personified, you'll soon be able to calm them down and have them eating out of your hand.

Attached Goats would do well to bring some of that lucky spontaneity into their relationship – particularly if you've been together a long time. Your love life would benefit from some spicing up and, being a creative Goat, you won't be short of ideas!

Use some of that extra cash to enjoy weekends away, romantic dinners, and days out or cosy, candlelit nights in. And don't be surprised if all that romance has tangible results. Many Goats will be welcoming a little kid into the family this year.

Secrets of Success in 2020

Goats are rarely materialistic types and, for people born under this sign, success often means tracking down some interesting, unusual, or very old piece of artwork or item; or finally completing an intricate creative project to Goat's own satisfaction.

Success is a very personal concept to Goats. In fact, success to a Goat can look very much like eccentricity to other signs. Yet, in 2020, the Goat's impression of success could, by pure chance, end up looking recognisably like the genuine article to other signs too.

This is because, in 2020, a creative Goat project could strike gold and everyone's going to notice that!

All Goat needs to do is continue working on it in an orderly, disciplined way. This is not as easy as it sounds as Goats, though hard-working when inspired, tend to be disorganised and impractical. This year, it's really important to get a grip, Goat. Master that and the sky's the limit.

The other important tip is to try to impose some structure on your finances. Consider creating a budget – quite a radical concept for Goats – and sticking to it. This will be to your advantage because while Rat years bring you money, the sneaky side of Rat nature also comes to the fore and some of that same increase could be stolen away or disappear.

Make a big effort to resist extravagant entertaining, buying too many generous gifts, and giving too lavishly to charity. These things are all wonderful to do, of course, but you need to think of the future. Stash some cash for leaner years and you'll be a much happier Goat.

The Goat Year at a Glance

January – A quiet start to the year. Let your imagination roam.

February – An exciting idea takes root. Start networking to increase your contacts.

March – The pace is accelerating. A new person enters the scene. They could bring you luck.

April – Work colleagues look at you with new eyes. Opportunity is in the air.

May – Time to treat yourself to a new image. New hair, new clothes – you need to look your best. You're attracting attention.

June – A friend wants you to join them on a break. If you can spare the time, why not?

July – Cash comes in, but an envious person may try to spoil your mood. Don't let them.

August – Everything's going well but energy may flag. Make time for rest and relaxation.

September – Social stars are shining. Romance is in the air.

October – At work, or in love, a protective person is looking after your interests.

November – Time to get out and about, and enjoy yourself.

December – Wealth is accumulating. Don't ignore those bills. Pay them off, reign in the Christmas spending, and look forward to a prosperous New Year.

Lucky Colours for 2020: Red, Green, Purple

Lucky Numbers for 2020: 2, 4, 9

CHAPTER 10: THE MONKEY

猴

Monkey Years

6 February 1932 – 25 January 1933

25 January 1944 – 12 February 1945

12 February 1956 – 30 January 1957

30 January 1968 – 16 February 1969

16 February 1980 – 4 February 1981

4 February 1992 – 22 January 1993

22 January 2004 – 8 February 2005

8 February 2016 – 27 January 2017

26 January 2028 – 12 February 2029

Natural Element: Metal

Will 2020 be a Golden year for the Monkey?

Good news, Monkey. It looks like this will be exactly the sort of year you like best! Agile, intelligent, and quick-thinking as you are, the one thing you can't stand is being bored; and if one quality – above all others – runs through 2020 like letters through a stick of rock, it's activity. Sparkling new activity, at that.

There will be mental stimulation everywhere you look, Monkey, and if you're typical of your sign, your first thought will be: 'Bring it on!'

The reason for Monkey's good fortune in 2020 is that the Monkey and the ruler of the year, the Rat, are terrific friends. They're different, admittedly, but they share so many complementary characteristics that they just click.

Neither Monkey nor Rat can bear standing still for long and when they move, which is often, the pace is swift. Unlike some other signs, Monkey can more than keep up with the busy Rat.

Last year probably started well for most Monkeys, as the Monkey and the merry Pig of 2019 get along amiably enough but – chances are – after a while the fun fizzled out. Many typical Monkeys started feeling bogged down with the Pig's endless pauses for refreshment, and before the year was out found themselves longing for a leaner, quicker, more streamlined approach.

Rat can provide all that... and then some.

What's more, the Rat belongs to the water element while the Monkey is a metal creature. These two elements are regarded as being in harmony. In fact, metal is believed to enhance and protect water so the Rat is grateful to Monkey and will help whenever possible.

There's even a chance you will go into business or join forces with someone born under the sign of the Rat, this year, Monkey. If you do, the venture will prosper. It might be worth checking out the birth signs of your friends and colleagues as soon as possible!

Career matters are favoured right now and it looks as if a hobby you enjoy will unexpectedly turn into a money-making business for you. 2020 is the year when promising seeds for the next decade or more are planted, so this enterprise could be something that starts small but will flourish astonishingly in years to come.

Excitingly, many Monkeys have a touch of stardust about them in 2020, and you'll get plenty of opportunities to show off your talents and dazzle an audience. Unlike more reticent signs, the Monkey is perfectly happy demonstrating unusual skills, making people laugh, or engaging in witty repartee. Even though you're quite capable of being quiet, you're not really shy, Monkey, and you secretly relish being the centre of attention.

Employed Monkeys can't afford to be lazy this year, or the usually supportive Rat will turn cranky on you. It would also be a good idea to try to be more of a team player. And before adopting that brilliant innovation you've just invented for the company, check with the boss first.

Chances are it will be greeted with enthusiasm, but this year the boss will demand to be consulted.

Get all this right, and you can make substantial gains financially, and in status, Monkey.

While this is not necessarily the perfect year to move home, many Monkeys will use some of their increased cash to make wise investments.

Travel looks well-starred, too. The restless Monkey loves to be on the move from place to place, and in 2020 travel for business or connected to your work in some way, will lead to financial gain.

All in all, 2020 has the makings of a great year for the Monkey. Just remember that even active Monkeys need some downtime too. Take yourself off into nature for some gentle relaxation as often as you can and you'll be in fine form to snap up all the goodies on offer.

What it Means to be a Monkey in 2020

There was a time when we tended to regard the Monkey as a figure of fun. The creature's awesome agility, effortless acrobatics, and natural clowning made us laugh and if they sensed an audience, the animals would show off shamelessly. Which, of course, only made us enjoy them more.

Yet, in China, the Monkey was credited with far more qualities than simply those of a born entertainer. The sign of the Monkey is associated with intelligence, justice, and wisdom. Behind those mischievous eyes the Chinese detected a shrewd brain and ability to plan the best course of action.

Like their namesakes, people born under the sign of Monkey tend to be physically agile. They're quick-moving, quick-thinking types with glittering wit and charismatic personalities. At a party, the Monkey will be in the centre of the group that's convulsed with laughter. Monkeys love jokes and humour of all kinds, and if anyone's going to start entertaining the crowd with a few magic tricks, it's likely to be a Monkey.

While not necessarily conventionally good-looking, the Monkey's lively face and sparkling eyes are always attractive and Monkeys have no difficulty in acquiring partners. The tricky bit for a Monkey is staying around long enough to build a relationship.

People born under this sign need constant mental stimulation. They don't necessarily expect others to provide it. They are quite happy to amuse themselves with puzzles, conundrums, the mending of broken objects, and inventing things, but they also need new places and new faces. Few signs can keep up with Monkey's constant motion.

What's more, Monkeys are not good with rules or authority. They've seldom seen a rule they don't want to break or avoid. In fact, it sometimes seems as if Monkey deliberately seeks out annoying regulations just for the fun of finding a way around them.

Yet, beneath the humour and games, the Monkey is ambitious with an astute brain. Monkeys can turn their hand to almost anything and make a success of it, but they're probably best-suited to working for themselves. If anyone is going to benefit from their efforts they believe it should be, chiefly, themselves. Also, they're not good at taking orders and, to be fair, they're so clever they don't need to. They can usually see the best way to carry out a task better than anyone else.

The Monkey home is often a work in progress. Monkey is always looking for a quicker, easier, cheaper, or more efficient way of doing everything and new ideas could encompass the entire building from the plumbing to the lighting and novel security systems. The first home in the street to be operated by remote control is likely to be the Monkey's. Yet, chances are, Monkey would prefer to meet friends in a nearby restaurant.

When it comes to holidays, Monkeys can have a bag packed seemingly in seconds, and are ready to be off anywhere, anytime. They don't much mind where they go as long as it's interesting, unusual, and offers plenty to be discovered. Lying on a sun-lounger for extended periods does not appeal.

Best Jobs for Monkey 2020

Inventor

Barrister

Magician

Journalist

Photographer

IT Expert

Perfect Partners

Cupid's arrow can strike anywhere at any time, of course, but once the novelty of new romance wears off, some relationships are easier to maintain than others. Here's a guide to the Monkey compatibility with other signs.

Monkey with Monkey

It's not always the case that opposites attract. More often like attracts like and when two Monkeys get together, they find each other delightful. At last, they've met another brain as quick and agile as their own and a person who relishes practical jokes as much as they do. What's more, this is a partner that shares a constant need for change and novelty. Yet, despite this, two Monkeys can often end up competing with each other. As long as they can recognise this, and laugh about it, they'll be fine.

Monkey with Rooster

While not a perfect match, these two have got a lot of time for each other. Monkey recognises the intelligent brain beneath Rooster's plumage while Rooster admires Monkey's ability to entertain a crowd and they both adore socialising. They could enjoy many fun dates together. Long-term, though, Rooster may tire of Monkey's jokes.

Monkey with Dog

Monkey finds Dog intriguing. Monkey senses Dog's strength of character coupled with its playful streak which fits well with Monkey's love of games. Dog, meanwhile, appreciates Monkey's energy and light-hearted approach. Yet, before long, Monkey's disdain for rules will grate on Dog's instinctive love of them. They cannot agree in this area, and it could lead to arguments.

Monkey with Pig

On the surface, these two might seem an unlikely couple. Yet Pig enjoys Monkey's fun and humour while Monkey is happy to be admired uncritically. What's more, Monkey's inventive mind can solve any difficulties caused by Pig's spending and since Monkey can't resist a challenge, the opportunity to retrain Pig, or at least find a way to obtain purchases cheaper, could help the relationship last.

Monkey with Rat

Unlikely as it might appear, mischievous Monkey and the clever Rat make a good partnership. Their quick minds, sociable natures, and love of novelty ensure that they're never bored together. True, Rat might sometimes feel that Monkey is too inclined to skim over the surface of things and could do with being more serious at times but Monkey's ingenuity and audaciousness always saves the day. Both can have a weakness for gambling though, so need to take care.

Monkey with Ox

The naughty Monkey scandalises Ox but in such an amusing way that Ox can't help laughing. Monkey, on the other hand, is equally amused to find an audience so easy to shock. This unlikely pair enjoy each other's company and get on surprisingly well. Yet, right from the start, it's probably obvious to both that a long-term relationship couldn't last. A fun flirtation, though, could be a terrific tonic for them both.

Monkey with Tiger

Tiger can't help being intrigued by sparkling Monkey and Monkey is flattered by such interest. Who wouldn't enjoy being admired by such a fabulous creature? But irrepressible Monkey just can't help teasing, and being teased is not a sensation Tiger is familiar with (or appreciates). Unless the attraction is very strong, these two will wind each other up until they can bear it no longer and part.

Monkey with Rabbit

Mercurial Monkey doesn't really 'get' Rabbit. The Monkey can appreciate how well Rabbit operates and sees this approach gets good results, but it's all too picky and slow for Monkey. Rabbit, on the other hand, is amused by Monkey's quick wit and clever ways but deplores Monkey's slapdash, sometimes devious tactics. Very unlikely to work out.

Monkey with Dragon

These two are likely to hit it off immediately. Each is attracted to the other's intelligence and lively presence, and Dragon's exuberance doesn't overwhelm hyperactive Monkey. What's more, although they both enjoy being surrounded by a crowd, Monkey only wants to make people laugh while Dragon hopes to inspire them to a cause. There is no conflict, so this couple can help each other to go far.

Monkey with Snake

These two clever creatures ought to admire each other, if only for their fine minds and, at first, it's possible they might. But unless they're really determined to make it work, it won't be long before active Monkey finds Snake's energy-saving ways irritating, while Snake loses patience with Monkey's endless jokes.

Monkey with Horse

Uh oh – best not attempted unless it's love at first sight. Monkey and Horse have wildly different outlooks and can't seem to see eye to eye on anything. They're both lively but in different ways that don't complement each other. Monkey will consider Horse's moods illogical and pointless while Horse is irritated that Monkey makes no attempt to understand how Horse feels. Very hard work.

Monkey with Goat

Monkey and Goat are different but in a good way. Though they don't quite 'get' each other deep down, Goat admires Monkey's lively personality and magical ability to come up with solutions for everything, while curious Monkey enjoys Goat's knowledge of the arts and the unusual. Long-term, Goat might not present enough of a challenge for Monkey but, with effort, it's a promising match.

Monkey Love 2020 Style

The year of the Rat is renowned for its socialising, and both single and attached Monkeys will delight in endless opportunities to be the centre of attention.

It makes no difference if the Monkey is married, or at least spoken for – flirting is part of the Monkey DNA and their loved ones will just have to get used to it.

Single Monkeys, however, can enjoy themselves with a clear conscience. It looks like you'll have a ball, Monkey. Several new partners could come and go, but you're unlikely to suffer. Whether the same could be said of them is debatable. Try to be kind, Monkey. You can't help being gorgeous and they'll miss you.

Just watch out for gossip. Certain jealous types envy your magnetism and could spread malicious rumours in an effort to dent your popularity. It won't work, of course, but it helps to be aware. It could turn out that someone you thought was a friend does not have your best interests at heart. They'll be sorry in the end, though.

Attached Monkeys have their usual dilemma – how to keep that Monkey restlessness at bay and stay settled with the same person. It's more important than ever to find an answer to this conundrum, Monkey, because it seems your partner could do with more support this year, and you're the one to provide it.

Dig deep to find those reserves of patience and sympathy. Yes, they're down there somewhere, Monkey! Then use that inventive mind of yours to dream up a variety of whacky hobbies to share, or places to visit, and the two of you could make 2020 your special year to remember.

Secrets of Success in 2020

There's nothing very secret about your success this year, Monkey. Success has got your name all over it. It's more a case of managing yourself and toning down those wild impulses for which you're famous – small things that could end up costing you dear in the long run, if you don't get them under control.

You benefit this year from helpful people who will appear to assist you, as if by magic, just when you need them most. This is a very fortunate piece of luck bestowed by the Rat, so don't take it for granted and make a point of being humble and grateful. Any hint of arrogance or over-confidence will backfire.

Not all of your supporters will be as quick and sharp as you, Monkey. Nevertheless it's important to be patient with them and listen respectfully.

One of the things about you that Rat doesn't care for so much, is your tendency to skimp on picky details and forget to finish a task properly. If you make a big effort to conquer this habit, Monkey, you'll find your projects will fly.

Finally, don't be tempted to get involved in any legal squabbles. Even if you think you've got the perfect case, chances are it will turn out to be far more complicated than you realised and end up costing a fortune. You may be provoked but try to smile sweetly and move on.

The Monkey Year at a Glance

January – Complete unfinished tasks from last year, and tidy up all details properly.

February – Learning a new skill suddenly appeals. Follow your instincts. It could prove profitable.

March – A tempting offer comes your way. Time to take a chance.

April – A false friend could be watching you closely; be on guard.

May – Don't let gossip dent your confidence. Stay calm. Keep doing what you're doing.

June – Your talents are getting the recognition they deserve. Take a bow!

July – Now you can come out and show everyone what you can do. You've got star quality.

August – Don't worry if your success attracts envy. You've got more admirers than critics.

September – Time to go travelling. You've earned a change of scene.

October – Cash is coming your way and romance is in the air. Just don't be too naughty.

November – Avoid reckless gambling but a tiny flutter shouldn't hurt. Luck is on your side.

December – People are packing up for the festivities but you're raring to go. Put your energy into partying instead, Monkey.

Lucky Colours for 2020: Yellow, Gold, White

Lucky Numbers for 2020: 2, 5, 9

CHAPTER 11: THE ROOSTER

雞

Rooster Years

26 January 1933 – 13 February 1934

13 February 1945 – 1 February 1946

31 January 1957 – 17 February 1958

17 February 1969 – 5 February 1970

5 February 1981 – 24 January 1982

23 January 1993 – 9 February 1994

9 February 2005 – 28 January 2006

28 January 2017 – 15 February 2018

13 February 2029 – 2 February 2030

Natural Element: Metal

Will 2020 be a Golden Year for the Rooster?

Stand by, Rooster. This could be a year you shout about – though perhaps not quite in the way you expect.

People born under the sign of the Rooster tend to be misunderstood. Their magnificent looks, opulent clothes, and confident manner suggests to other signs that this is a creature obsessed with wealth – or at least an individual who puts the pursuit of prosperity at the top of their list of priorities.

Yet, this idea is not strictly true. Roosters strive for lovely things simply to impress other signs into appreciating them. They're not particularly interested in amassing money, or even status, for their own sake. Deep down, they just want to be loved.

So, 2020 could mark a happy turning point for the Rooster, or at least a fresh start on a better footing.

Last year, when the indulgent zodiac Pig ruled the roost, Rooster could afford to sit back a little and let things slide. In 2020, it's a different story. Now, Rooster is going to have to wake up, get back into the farmyard and start doing the job he was built for.

The reason is, unlike the Pig, the Rat doesn't view the Rooster uncritically. Rat actually admires a great deal about his feathered colleague but also disapproves of loud ways and any behaviour that smacks of bragging.

On the other hand, Rat thoroughly applauds a smart appearance, so this year the Rooster can expect plenty of cash to fund an extensive wardrobe or a fancy car.

What's more, few realise what a family-oriented creature the Rooster can be. Roosters have immense loyalty to their families though they may not always show it.

This is where Rooster and Rat are definitely on the same wavelength. The Rat puts family first when it comes to spending and will support the Rooster with any projects that benefit the Rooster brood.

Consequently, any ventures Rooster undertakes with family members will blossom. It's likely, too, that the Rooster will be called upon to help certain people in the family circle, financially, throughout the year. Oddly enough, though a lot of cash is likely to disappear in this direction, the more generously Rooster provides, the more the Rooster bank balance is later boosted.

Giving to the right causes will actually increase Rooster prosperity this year. In fact, the more the Rooster thinks of other people, even those outside the family circle, and tries to help, the more luck will come Rooster's way.

The Rat is a water creature while the Rooster belongs to the metal element. These two elements are believed to work harmoniously together which is why Rooster and Rat get on well in many ways. Metal is reckoned to nurture water and the element of the year is also metal.

This could mean that the Rooster is called upon to do a great deal of encouraging, assisting, and general supporting throughout 2020. Your phone may never stop ringing with cries for help, Rooster, and work colleagues could be endlessly needing your attention.

In one way, you may welcome the warm feeling this gives you. You'll certainly know you're wanted. But all that energy you're forced to expend could leave you drained and exhausted. It would be a good plan to book some relaxing holidays as early as possible.

Though your focus is likely to be on others this year, Rooster, rather than climbing the career ladder you could find you get a sudden and unexpected boost at work. It's likely to come right out of the blue. The company you work for could get taken over and Rooster is catapulted surprisingly to the top of the new regime. Or someone could dramatically leave, or retire, causing the efficient Rooster to be asked to step into their shoes.

However it happens, Rooster, without actively seeking it out, you may find you're offered a lucrative promotion.

It looks as if many Roosters have endured a long spell during which most of their personal relationships haven't brought them as much satisfaction as they would have liked.

In 2020, the balance can finally be restored. Though most aspects of the Rooster life will be improving, chances are, the area that benefits greatest concerns love and affection. And for all your fine feathers, Rooster, that's what will mean the most.

What it means to be a Rooster in 2020

Colourful, bold, and distinctly noisy, the Rooster rules the farmyard. Seemingly fearless and relishing the limelight, this bird may be small but he doesn't appear to know it. We're looking at a giant personality here. This creature may be the bane of late sleepers, and only a fraction of the size of other animals on the farm, but the Rooster doesn't care. Rooster struts around, puffing out his tiny chest as if he owns the place.

The Chinese associate the Rooster with courage and it's easy to see why. You'd have to be brave to square up to all-comers armed only with a modest beak, a couple of sharp claws, and a piercing shriek. Yet, Rooster is quite prepared to take on the challenge.

People born in the year of the Rooster tend to be gorgeous to look at, and like to dress flamboyantly. Even if their physique is not as slender as it could be, the Rooster is not going to hide it away in drab, black outfits. Roosters enjoy colour and style, and they dress to be noticed. These are not shy retiring types. They like attention and they do whatever they can to get it.

Roosters are charming and popular with quick minds and engaging repartee. They have to guard against a tendency to boast but this happens mainly when they sense a companion's interest is wandering.

And since they're natural raconteurs, they can usually recapture attention and pass their stories off as good entertainment.

Like the feathered variety, Roosters can be impetuous and impulsive. They tend to rush into situations and commitments that are far too demanding, without a second thought and then, later on, wonder frantically how they're going to manage. Oddly enough, they usually make things work but only after ferocious effort. Roosters just can't help taking a risk.

Although they're gregarious and often surrounded by friends, there's a sense that – deep down – few people know the real Rooster. Underneath the bright plumage and cheerful banter, Rooster is quite private and a little vulnerable. Perhaps Roosters fear they'll disappear or get trampled on if they don't make enough noise. So they need frequent reassurance that they're liked and appreciated.

With all the emphasis Rooster puts on the splendid Rooster appearance, it's often overlooked that, in fact, the Rooster has a good brain and is quite a thinker. Roosters keep up with current affairs, they're shrewd with money and business matters, and though you never see them doing it, in private they're busily reading up on all the latest information on their particular field.

At work, Rooster wants to be the boss and often ends up that way. Failing that, Roosters will go it alone and start their own business. They're usually successful due to the Rooster's phenomenal hard work but when things do go wrong it's likely to be down to the Rooster's compulsion to take a risk or promise more than it's possible to deliver. Also, while being sensitive to criticism, themselves, Roosters can be extremely frank in putting across their views to others. They may pride themselves on their plain-speaking but it may not do them any favours with customers and employees.

Rooster thinks the home should be a reflection of its owner's splendid image so, if at all possible, it will be lavish, smart, and full of enviable items. They have good taste, in a colourful way, and don't mind spending money on impressive pieces. If the Rooster can be persuaded to take a holiday, a five-star hotel in a prestigious location with plenty of socialising would be ideal, or a luxury cruise with a place at the Captain's Table.

Best Jobs for Rooster

Managing Director

Fashion Buyer

Mayor

M.P.

The Military (Officer Level)

Hairdresser

Make-up Artist

Theatre Director

Perfect Partners

Cupid's arrow can strike anywhere at any time, of course, but once the novelty of new romance wears off, some relationships are easier to maintain than others. Here's a guide to the Rooster's compatibility with other signs.

Rooster with Rooster

Fabulous to look at though they would be, these two alpha creatures would find it difficult to share the limelight. They can't help admiring each other at first sight but since both needs to be the boss, there could be endless squabbles for dominance. What's more, neither would be able to give the other the regular reassurance they need. Probably not worth attempting.

Rooster with Dog

Rooster and Dog are not the best of partners. Dog can be as plain-spoken as Rooster and is not likely to be impressed by overt show. What's more, Dog is often critical and Rooster can't stand criticism. Rooster, on the other hand, is likely to sense and resent Dog's attitude. Frustration abounds for both in this relationship. Only for the hopelessly love-struck.

Rooster with Pig

These two might seem an unlikely couple – modest Pig with extrovert Rooster. Yet Pig has no need or wish to crow and can see the vulnerable character that lurks beneath Rooster's fine feathers; Rooster, meanwhile, responds to Pig's kindness and undemanding nature. As long as Rooster doesn't get bored, this can be a contented relationship.

Rooster with Rat

The first thing Rat notices about the Rooster is its beautiful plumage, but this is a relationship which is unlikely to get much further than initial admiration. Rooster's direct and frank approach can strike the Rat as tactless, while the Rooster can't understand why Rat has to make life so convoluted and complicated. Then again, Rooster's natural confidence and aplomb can come across as bragging to the Rat. These two have to be very determined to make a partnership work.

Rooster with Ox

For all its bravado and showing off, the Rooster is a down-to-earth type, drawn to security and accumulating the good things in life – requirements that Ox understands very well and can supply effortlessly. What's more, Ox can't help but admire Rooster's fine feathers and skill at communicating in a crowd – attributes Ox doesn't have and is unlikely to acquire. These two could enjoy a very good partnership.

Rooster with Tiger

The only feathered creature in the zodiac, the opulence and novelty of Rooster's appearance will draw Tiger like a magnet. What's more, deep down they are both quite serious-minded types so on one level they'll have much to share. Yet, despite this, they're not really on the same wavelength and misunderstandings will keep recurring. Could be hard work.

Rooster with Rabbit

A difficult match. However unfair it seems, Rooster comes over as loud, boastful, and uncouth to Rabbit while Rabbit appears dull, staid, and insufficiently admiring of Rooster's fine feathers to appeal to Rooster. These two just can't see below the surface of the other and it would be surprising if they ended up together. Only to be considered by the very determined.

Rooster with Dragon

A Dragon and Rooster pairing will always attract attention. These two are both gorgeous beings and love to be surrounded by admirers. They will probably enjoy going out together and being seen as a couple, but in the long-term they may not be able to provide the kind of support each secretly needs. Entertaining for a while but probably not a lasting relationship.

Rooster with Snake

Surprisingly, Snake and Rooster work well together. Both gorgeous in different ways, they complement each other without competing. Snake's keen eyes can see beneath Rooster's proud facade to the sensitive, unsure person inside, while Rooster appreciates Snake's unobtrusive strength and wise words of encouragement at just the right moment. These two could be inseparable.

Rooster with Horse

The eye-catching Rooster intrigues Horse while Rooster appreciates Horse's strength and agility. They can enjoy many stimulating dates together. Yet, in the long-run, this couple may not be able to provide the stability the other needs. They're both sensitive types but in different ways. After a while, the relationship could run out of steam.

Rooster with Goat

Peaceful Goat is not one to make feathers fly, so these two are unlikely to fall out, but they're unlikely to find perfect compatibility either. Goat is unable to give Rooster the regular ego boosts that make Rooster thrive while Rooster is baffled by Goat's unpredictable devotion to impractical projects or people. Misunderstandings are likely.

Rooster with Monkey

While not a perfect match, these two have got a lot of time for each other. Monkey recognises the intelligent brain beneath Rooster's plumage while Rooster admires Monkey's ability to entertain a crowd and they both adore socialising. They could enjoy many fun dates together. Long-term, though, Rooster may tire of Monkey's jokes.

Rooster Love 2020 Style

The wonderful side-effect of putting family and friends first this year, Rooster, is that they're so pleased with you, they want you at all their gatherings and celebrations. Chances are you'll be guest of honour, too.

This means that all Roosters – single and attached – will have countless opportunities to strut their stuff in 2020. What's more, another side-effect of a Rat year is that the Rat somehow has magical qualities that make Roosters look even more lovely than usual.

The Rooster is going to be a highly desirable catch in 2020. Yet, strangely enough, despite loving the attention and courting even more, the Rooster isn't easy to snare.

For all that showy plumage and careless talk, Roosters have high ideals when it comes to love. They only give their hearts to the most special of admirers. Yet this year, Rooster, that very rare someone could just breeze into your life – particularly at a family occasion.

Attached Roosters will get more pleasure than usual from snuggling up with their partners at home. That's not to say you won't enjoy partying and surrounding yourself with a crowd – you are a Rooster after all – but for once you're highly appreciative of domestic bliss. Just keep a guard on that tactless tongue. Plain speaking is all very well, but not over a candlelit supper.

Secrets of Success

Putting other people's interests before your own is the biggest secret of success for you in 2020, Rooster. And if you're investing in your family you'll be even luckier.

Fortunate events will enhance your career, but they appear to have little to do with your current input. They seem to arrive unbidden as a result of your past efforts, coupled with a surprise move on the part of someone else.

However it happens though, Rooster, you can happily accept your gains, offer up a little prayer of thanks, and then think about putting them to good use.

Once again, it's very important to restrain your more extravagantly Rooster-ish traits. The ones that can irritate other signs at times. You know what we're talking about, Rooster! You don't mean to boast when you've done something brilliant but that's how your excited and frequently-repeated accounts of your exploits often come across to others.

Be aware, too, that you're very susceptible to flattery and this year an unscrupulous person could use this tendency to try to take advantage of you. If the praise seems over-the-top, Rooster, it probably is. So stop lapping it up, and ask yourself what they want.

The Rooster Year at a Glance

January – The New Year arrives with good fortune. You're feeling optimistic.

February – Be careful not to gossip. Envious rivals could twist what you say.

March – Make an early start as spring arrives. You can accomplish much.

April – Someone needs your help. Give generously. Not necessarily money; could be time and attention.

May – Tricky for Roosters – tact and diplomacy are called for. Count to ten and make nice.

June – Your efforts are attracting attention in a good way. Tangible rewards coming to you.

July – Intriguing news reaches your ears. Find out if it's true before passing it on.

August – Summer parties, family gatherings, and all-round good fun on the agenda. Enjoy.

September – Good deeds are being recognised. Step forward and accept deserved praise.

October – Take extra care around machinery and on the road. Accidents can happen.

November – Angry voices disturb your peace. Keep out of it, Rooster.

December – You will look back over the year with satisfaction, and your popularity is at an all-time high.

Lucky Colours 2020: Purple, Red, Brown

Lucky Numbers 2020: 7, 8

CHAPTER 12: THE DOG

狗

Dog Years

14 February 1934 – 3 February 1935

2 February 1946 – 21 January 1947

18 February 1958 – 7 February 1959

6 February 1970 – 26 January 1971

25 January 1982 – 12 February 1983

10 February 1994 – 30 January 1995

29 January 2006 – 17 February 2007

16 February 2018 – 4 February 2019

Natural Element: Metal

Will 2020 be a Golden Year for the Dog?

Well, Dog, did you know you were born under an auspicious sign? So much so, the Chinese used to believe that if an unknown dog visited a house, it foretold a coming fortune to the lucky family that lived there.

That being the case, you're bound to have a good year in 2020, and people will be delighted to see you wherever you go.

There will be a few ups and downs, of course, mainly because the Dog and the Rat, while getting on tolerably enough don't quite gel on every level.

This slight friction between your energy and the Rat energy of the year could lead to misunderstandings blowing up out of nowhere and unco-operative people getting in your way, or seemingly blocking your path, Dog.

Being a tenacious canine, of course, you'll have no trouble either chasing them away or forging a course right through them, but it's annoying and time-wasting to have to bother.

Whereas last year, the luxury-loving year of the Pig allowed you to slow down a tad and indulge your inner puppy, this year suggests a return to the conscientious, serious-minded approach you do so well.

The fact is, one of the main areas where Dog and Rat see eye to eye is the belief in the importance of hard work and sustained effort. The Rat can be very demanding where this subject is concerned and – in Rat years – an increased workload is to be expected right around the zodiac.

Yet, as a Dog, you remain undaunted. You have great stamina and a responsible attitude, so the extra duties likely to come your way in 2020 present no problem at all.

In fact, oddly, you may find this year that you have more than one job. Not in the sense that you change jobs during the year – though you might – but more that you'll be juggling several interesting career roles at the same time.

Rat is a water creature while Dog belongs to the metal element and these elements are in harmony. Another good sign. Traditionally, water suggests money flowing towards you and those Dogs working several jobs at once, at the very least, can expect a boost in income – although a boost in status and esteem could well materialise, too.

Yet, this year, Dogs are prone to finding cash slipping through their paws rather too easily. Even though you've earned it fair and square, resist the temptation to spend too freely. It will be difficult to save but if you manage to hang on to your money, you could end the year wealthy.

Friends play a big part in Dog fortune in 2020. Dogs are traditionally co-operative, pack animals, which are skilled in working together as a team. This year, in particular, a team effort will be especially beneficial, multiplying your success many times over.

The Rat, after all, also likes to hang out with a tribe of fellow Rats, so group activities are favoured over solo acts in the coming months.

Many Dogs will be thinking about property this year, and possibly moving home. Curiously, it seems as if even though you may settle on a new place in the next few months, Dog, you won't actually move in until next year. This may be because a lot of building and decorating work needs to be done before it's ready for you, or perhaps there's some sort of delay over contracts; for whatever reason, there looks to be a gap between making your decision and actually taking action.

Whatever happens, though, don't be lured into legal action. The Dog is the most honest of signs and is passionate about fairness and justice. You can also be stubborn, Dog. So when you reckon you've been wronged, you find it difficult to rest until equity is restored – you just won't give up. You know what they say about a dog and a bone.

Yet, chances are, it will do you no good this year. No matter how water-tight you think your case is, Dog, weasel words can twist the facts until you end up either losing or winning, but near bankrupting yourself in the process.

Just don't go there, Dog.

Finally, though strong and resilient, Dogs are also born worriers and the lively but changeable energy this year could play havoc with your nerves. Take care to insist on as many holidays and open-air breaks as you can fit in, Dog, and you can thrive in 2020.

What it means to Be a Dog in 2020

Though some cultures are quite rude about the dog, and regard the very name as a disparaging term, in the West we tend to be rather sentimental about our canine friends.

The Chinese, on the other hand, while regarding the zodiac Dog with respect, discern more weighty qualities in the faithful hound. They regard the sign of the Dog as representing justice and compassion. People born under the sign of the Dog, therefore, are admired for their noble natures and fair-minded attitudes.

Typical Dogs will do the right thing, even if it means they'll lose out personally. They have an inbuilt code of honour that they hate to break.

The Dog is probably the most honest sign of the zodiac. People instinctively trust the Dog even if they don't always agree with Dog's opinions. Yet Dogs are usually completely unaware of the high esteem in which they're held, because they believe they're only acting naturally; doing what anyone else would do in the circumstances.

Since they have such a highly-developed sense of right and wrong, Dogs understand the importance of rules. Also, since deep down they're always part of a pack – even if it's invisible – Dogs know that fairness is vital. If there aren't fair shares all round, there's likely to be trouble they believe. So, to keep the peace, Dog knows that a stout framework of rules is required and once set up, everyone should stick to them. Dogs are genuinely puzzled that other signs can't seem to grasp this simple truth!

People born under this sign tend to be physically strong with thick, glossy hair, and open, friendly faces. Their warm manner attracts new acquaintances but they tend to stay acquaintances for quite a while. It takes a long time for Dog to promote a person from acquaintance to real friend. This is because Dogs are one hundred percent loyal and will never let a friend down, so they don't give their trust lightly.

Dogs are intelligent and brave, and once they've made up their mind, they stick to it. They're quite prepared to go out on a limb for a good cause if necessary, but they don't really like being alone. They're much happier in a group, with close friends or family. What's more, though they're good managers, they're not interested in being in overall charge. They'd much rather help someone else achieve a goal than take all the responsibility themselves.

At work, Dog can be a puzzle to the boss. Though capable of immense effort, and obviously the dedicated type, it's difficult to enthuse the Dog. Promises of pay rises and promotion have little effect. The Dog is just not materialistic or particularly ambitious in the conventional sense. Yet, if a crisis appears, if someone's in trouble or disaster threatens, the Dog is suddenly energised and springs into action. In fact, it's quite difficult to hold Dog back. Dogs will work tirelessly, without rest or thought of reward, until the rescue is achieved.

Bearing this in mind, Dogs would do well to consider a career that offers some kind of humanitarian service. This is their best chance of feeling truly fulfilled and happy at work.

At home, Dogs have a down to earth approach. Home and stability are very important to them. They're not the types to keep moving and trading up, but at the same time they don't need their home to be a showcase. The Dog residence will be comfortable rather than stylish with the emphasis on practicality. Yet, it will have a warm, inviting atmosphere, and the favoured visitors permitted to join the family there will be certain of a friendly welcome.

It's not easy to get Dog to take a break if there's a cause to be pursued, but when Dogs finally allow themselves to come off-duty, they love to play. They like to be out in the open air or splashing through water, and can discover their competitive streak when it comes to team games.

Best Jobs for Dog

Charity Worker

Nurse

Doctor

Teacher

Security Guard

Policeman

Fireman

Bank Clerk

Perfect Partners

Cupid's arrow can strike anywhere at any time, of course, but once the novelty of new romance wears off, some relationships are easier to maintain than others. Here's a guide to the Dog compatibility with other signs.

Dog with Dog

Dogs love company so these two will gravitate to each other and stay there. Both loyal, faithful types, neither need worry the other will stray. They'll appreciate their mutual respect for doing things properly and their shared love of a stable, caring home. This relationship is likely to last and last. The only slight hitch could occur if, over time, the romance dwindles and Dog and Dog become more like good friends than lovers.

Dog with Pig

In the outside world, the Dog and the Pig can get along well together; in fact, Pigs being intelligent creatures can do many of the things dogs can do, so it's not surprising this zodiac pair make a good couple. Good natured Pig is uncomplicated and fair-minded which suits Dog perfectly. Also, Pig brings out Dog's playful side – which delights Pig who's always keen to have a playmate. A happy relationship involving many restaurants.

Dog with Rat

The Rat and the Dog get along pretty well together. Both strong characters, they respect each other and give each other space when required. But deep down, the Dog is a worrier and gets anxious about unnecessary risks, while Rat just can't help sailing close to the wind if an interesting opportunity presents itself. Long-term, reckless Rat might unintentionally drive Dog to distraction. Only to be considered by Dogs with nerves of steel.

Dog with Ox

These two ought to get along well as they're both sensible, down to earth, loyal, and hardworking, and in tune with each other's basic beliefs. And yet, somehow they don't. Dog has a playful streak and finds this lacking in Ox, while Ox may be baffled by what seems like pointless silliness in Dog. If they can agree to differ, they could make a relationship work.

Dog with Tiger

While not exactly opposites, these two are different enough to intrigue each other yet similar enough in basic outlook to get on well. Both Tiger and Dog are idealistic and uninterested in material gain yet where Dog can be nervous, Tiger's bold. And where Tiger attracts controversy, Dog will be loyal. This partnership could be lasting and valuable.

Dog with Rabbit

Despite the fact that in the outside world Rabbit could easily end up as Dog's dinner, the astrological pair gets on surprisingly well. Dog appreciates Rabbit's careful, efficient ways and soft voice, while Rabbit admires Dog's energy and good intentions. Dog's lack of interest in the finer points of interior design might try Rabbit's patience but with a little work, these two could reach an understanding.

Dog with Dragon

Not the easiest of combinations. Down-to-earth Dog can't see what all the fuss is about when it comes to Dragons. Unimpressed by glamour and irritated by what seems to Dog the gullibility of Dragon admirers, Dog can't be bothered to find out more. Dragon meanwhile, is hurt by Dog's lack of interest. Great determination would be needed to make this work.

Dog with Snake

Some snakes seem to have an almost hypnotic power, and for some reason Dog is particularly susceptible to these skills. We've heard of snake-charmers but snakes can be dog-charmers and without even trying, Snakes can find themselves the recipients of Dog devotion. Since the Dog is strong, loyal, and can be fun, Snake is not averse to this but might, in the end, find it boring.

Dog with Horse

Both good friends of man, these two can make a formidable team. Dog understands the occasional need for solitude while admiring Horse's strength and agility. Horse, meanwhile, senses Dog's loyalty and down to earth nature. Both lovers of the great outdoors and physical activity, they'll never be short of adventures to share. A promising long-term relationship.

Dog with Goat

This is another relationship that could be tricky. Loyal Dog would be quite willing to stand by Goat when practical problems loom but could end up irritated by Goat's inability to learn from previous mistakes and so keeps making them. Goat can't understand why Dog gets so bothered. With care, these two could learn to live together.

Dog with Monkey

Monkey finds Dog intriguing. Monkey senses Dog's strength of character coupled with its playful streak which fits well with Monkey's love of games. Dog, meanwhile, appreciates Monkey's energy and light-hearted approach. Yet before long, Monkey's disdain for rules will grate on Dog's instinctive love of them. They cannot agree in this area, and it could lead to arguments.

Dog with Rooster

Rooster and Dog are not the best of partners. Dog can be as plain-spoken as Rooster and is not likely to be impressed by overt show. What's more, Dog is often critical and Rooster can't stand criticism. Rooster, on the other hand, is likely to sense and resent Dog's attitude. Frustration abounds for both in this relationship. Only for the hopelessly love-struck.

Dog Love 2020 Style

Love is in the air all you lucky Dogs and single Dogs could be enjoying something very special this year. If you've never believed in love at first sight 2020 could give you cause to change your mind.

You might not set out expecting to find the ONE, but some apparently insignificant evening or event could find you gazing across a crowded room and locking eyes with someone dazzling. You can take it from there Dog and it won't disappoint.

Attached Dogs can look forward to a peaceful and happy year with their other half though certain family members might butt in to cause a few ripples. A squabbling pack could cause irritation and even lead to arguments between you and your beloved, Dog so don't let it happen. Put a stop to the discord before it gets out of hand.

Make an effort to keep your temper, remain calm and if possible, escort the warring parties off your patch.

Secrets of Success

You are blessed with all the qualities you need to reap rich rewards from the coming year, Dog. Hard work, quick action, and steady progress come naturally to you, as does being a team player and interacting with friends.

More difficult for Dog, though, is the need to listen to other people's suggestions and to resist the temptation to cling stubbornly to your own way of doing things, because that's the way things have always been done.

At the beginning of a new cycle, fresh ideas are coming to the fore and the people who'll benefit are the ones who give them a chance to grow and flourish.

Listen and then innovate, Dog. Originality is what counts this year. It's time to be a leader not a follower.

And, finally, there are the pesky signs all around that keep trying to shove you off-course with their silly squabbles. Some you can defuse, but others you must walk away from. Rise above them, Dog, and carry on regardless.

The Dog Year at a Glance

January – Things may seem a little slow, but you're beginning to sense something good is happening.

February – Work is getting interesting. An important person is taking an interest in you. There could be beneficial repercussions.

March – New friends are joining your circle – possibly colleagues who have become closer. Work and play begin to mix.

April – An authority figure can be a pain. They may not deserve respect, but remain tactful. Speaking bluntly could cause trouble.

May – A fascinating new face enlivens the love scene. Time to explore where this romance could lead.

June – Summer skies are calling. An excellent time to take a break with a special person.

July – Romance is going well. Watch out for a colleague or neighbour who loves to cause complications.

August – Another good time for a holiday or short break. Someone close may be breaking the rules. They may not listen to your good advice.

September – A rival at work could be trying to claim the credit that belongs to you. Skilful tactics are required.

October – Peace is restored, yet you may be feeling restless. House hunting or shopping for a new image is favoured.

November – Fun and games are on the menu. You're in the mood to party.

December – Festivities are hotting up, yet your to-do list is getting longer. Keep calm.

Lucky Colours for 2020: Grey, Black, Blue

Lucky Numbers for 2020: 2, 6

CHAPTER 13: THE PIG

豬

Pig Years

4 February 1935 – 23 January 1936

22 January 1947 – 9 February 1948

8 February 1959 – 27 January 1960

27 January 1971 – 14 February 1972

13 February 1983 – 1 February 1984

31 January 1995 – 18 February 1996

18 February 2007 – 6 February 2008

5 February 2019 – 24 January 2020

Natural Element: Water

Will 2020 be a Golden Year for the Pig?

So here we are, Pig, at the end of your very own year, looking out on a fresh start. Chances are you're not too sad to say goodbye to 2019, and the Year of the Pig.

While it sounds like a huge advantage to be in charge for 12 whole months, the privilege has its drawbacks. For a start, you're not keen on too much responsibility. Then there are all those lessons the anniversary of your birth year requires you to learn. Good for you in the long run, of course, but not necessarily enjoyable at the time.

Well, now, you've come through it all a much wiser Pig no doubt, and found yourself face to face with the Rat.

The good news, Pig, is that the Rat is very fond of you so this should be a good year, and it will get better and better as the weeks go on. The second half of the year, in particular, is set to be your best time.

Right from the start, though, you'll notice a wonderful sense of freedom. At the time you probably weren't too aware of the responsibility associated with your birth year, but now it's gone – it's like a big weight has been lifted from your shoulders.

Suddenly, even more friends than usual are getting in touch and, at work, colleagues are only too glad to assist and encourage you any way you want. Even the boss seems eager to help, which for some Pigs looks almost miraculous.

Just don't be tempted to use this happy state of affairs as an excuse to slacken off, put your feet on the desk, and play with your phone. The Rat disapproves of laziness and a frivolous attitude towards work. Maintain a good pace and the rewards will flow.

In fact, it looks as if you will be branching out in a new direction career-wise, Pig. Some Pigs will continue with their current role while they explore something different in their spare time; others will take the plunge and embark on a complete change immediately.

However you do it, Pig, it looks as if by the time the year's out you'll be operating in a brand new field of some sort. As long as you put the effort in, the venture looks destined for success.

Like the Rat, you're a water creature, so you understand each other deep down and you both share a happy knack of flowing smoothly around any obstacles that appear in your path. Yet, since water also represents money in Chinese astrology, when the two of you get together there can be something of a flood.

Cash may flow in with welcome rapidity but it is likely to flow out just as fast or even faster. What's more, since (as an exuberant Pig) you love to spend while the canny Rat prefers to haggle for a bargain wherever possible, the two of you could fall out over finances.

In day to day life, this could take the form of debts beginning to build up, accompanied by stern letters from credit companies, or legal disputes over money, or even investments that go wrong.

Best not to treat yourself quite as often as you'd like, Pig. You'll be very glad if you manage restraint because if you can hang onto that flow of cash, you'll be amazed how wealthy you'll feel by Christmas.

You can also build up some good Karma in this area by doing good deeds and giving to charity whenever the opportunity arises.

One of the luckiest and happiest moments of your year seems to centre around a big family celebration. It could be a wedding, the arrival of a new baby, or the marking of an honour of some kind – but whatever it is, good fortune will pour your way as a result.

The only thing to slow you down, Pig, is your tendency to be enjoying your work so much this year that you forget to take time off. No point in wearing yourself out; as a typical Pig you can think of a million ways to wind down. How about a few days at a spa to start you off, and take it from there, Pig?

What it Means to Be a Pig in 2020

It takes quite a confident person in the West to announce 'I'm a Pig' to an assembled gathering without embarrassment. Imagine the comments! And if they should happen to be at an event where food is being served, they'd never hear the end of the jokes.

Yet, if you were in China and came out with such a remark, chances are you'd get a very favourable response. You'd certainly not be a figure of fun.

The Chinese zodiac Pig – sometimes known as the Boar – is regarded as a lucky sign. Since flesh and blood pigs tend to have very large litters of baby piglets, they're believed to be a symbol of prosperity and plenty.

And given the Chinese fondness for pork, anyone who owned a pig or two would have been fortunate indeed.

What's more, people born in any Year of the Pig tend to be genuinely amiable types – perhaps the most well-liked of all the 12 signs of the zodiac. Cheerful, friendly, and lacking in ego, they have no enemies. They can fit in anywhere. Nobody objects to a Pig.

Pigs just can't help being kind, sympathetic, and tolerant. Should someone let them down, Pigs will just shrug and insist it wasn't their fault. Pigs tend to get let down over and over again by the same people, but it never occurs to them to bear a grudge. They forgive and forget and move happily along. Friends may scold and warn them not to be a soft touch, but Pigs can't help it. They see no point in conflict.

That's not to say it's impossible to annoy a Pig, just that it takes a great deal to rouse the sweet Pig's nature to anger.

The other refreshing thing about the Pig is that they just want to be happy and have a good time – and they usually do. They find fun in the most unpromising situations, and their enthusiasm is infectious. Soon, everyone else is having fun too.

It's true Pigs enjoy their food – perhaps a little too much – but that's because they are a sensuous sign, appreciating physical pleasures; and it makes them very sexy too.

Shopping is a favourite hobby of many Pigs. They're not greedy, they just love spending money on pretty things simply for the sheer delight of discovering a new treasure and taking it home. This sometimes gets the Pig into trouble because finance isn't a strong point, but such is Pig's charm, they usually get away with it.

Pigs don't tend to be madly ambitious. They have no interest in the rat-race yet they are intelligent and conscientious and can't help being highly effective at work, despite having no ulterior motive or game plan. They often end up in managerial roles. Their sympathetic and conciliatory approach, coupled with their willingness to ask others for advice, goes down well in most organisations and usually leads to promotion. What's more, while avoiding unpleasantness wherever possible, the Pig doesn't like to give up on a task once started, and will invariably find a way to get it done that other signs wouldn't have thought of.

The Pig home reflects the sensuous nature of the Pig. Everything will be comfortable and warm with fabrics and furnishings that feel good as well as look good. Items will be chosen for ease of use rather than style, and there will probably be a great many objects and knick-knacks dotted around, picked up on Pig's shopping expeditions. Pigs quite often excel at cooking and the Pig kitchen is likely to be crammed with all the latest gadgets and devices for food preparation.

Pigs approve of holidays, of course, and take as many as they can. They're not desperate to tackle extreme sports or go on dangerous expeditions, but they can be adventurous too. They like to be out in the open air, especially if it involves picnics and barbecues but, basically, easy-going Pig's just happy to take a break.

Best Jobs for Pig

Cook

Restaurant Owner

Receptionist

Spa Therapist

Wedding Planner

Charity Worker

Perfect Partners

Cupid's arrow can strike anywhere at any time, of course, but once the novelty of new romance wears off, some relationships are easier to maintain than others. Here's a guide to the Pig's compatibility with other signs.

Pig with Pig

When one Pig sets eyes on another Pig, they can't help moving closer for a better look, and should they get talking they probably won't stop. These two understand each other and share so many interests and points of view they seem like a perfect couple. Yet, long-term, they can end up feeling too alike. Pigs rarely argue, yet oddly enough they can find themselves squabbling over trivialities with another Pig. Care needed.

Pig with Rat

It's very easy for Rat to be beguiled by the Pig. Pig's easy-going, sympathetic nature immediately relaxes the Rat. What's more, Pig loves shopping as much as Rat so the two of them could enjoy many happy expeditions together. Conflict could occur through overspending. Pig does not understand Rat's compulsion to bag a bargain. Pig will buy whatever the price and the two could end up arguing over money.

Pig with Ox

Delightful Pig will catch Ox's eye, and since Pig isn't a constant thrill-seeker, the two of them could enjoy many peaceful evenings together perhaps over a tasty meal. Yet Pig's spendthrift ways – at least in Ox's eyes – could soon prove very annoying as well as illogical to the Ox, while Pig could find Ox's attitude judgemental and upsetting. Not ideal for the long-term.

Pig with Tiger

Carefree Pig will love to bask in Tiger's impressive aura, while Tiger will feel good about protecting this charming but unworldly creature. They enjoy each other's company and Tiger, so focused on lofty matters, will find Pig's compulsive shopping too trivial to worry about. This couple could do well together as long as Pig's fondness for cosy nights in doesn't make Tiger feel trapped.

Pig with Rabbit

Pig is not quite as interested in fine dining as Rabbit, and is happy to scoff a burger as much as a cordon bleu creation, but their shared love of the good things in life makes these two happy companions. Once again, Pig's spending habits might irritate Rabbit, but not too much as Rabbit is quite willing to splurge on lovely things for the home. A relationship would work well.

Pig with Dragon

While Dragon and Pig might seem to be opposites, the two of them can create a surprisingly contented relationship. Pig is quite happy for Dragon to fly around doing exciting things as long as Pig is not expected to do much more than admire profusely. Dragon appreciates Pig's uncritical support and makes allowances for Pig's lack of stamina. This couple could live in harmony.

Pig with Snake

Pig and Snake don't have a lot to say to each other. Snake can't be bothered with Pig's endless shopping, and Pig is hurt by Snake's snobbish attitude. They both enjoy the good things in life so a luxury fling could briefly be fun – a shared spa break might be a good idea – but in the long-term, this relationship is probably not worth pursuing.

Pig with Horse

Pig and Horse are good companions. Horse is soothed by easy-going Pig and Pig is proud to be seen with such an alluring creature as Horse. They don't have a lot of interests in common but they don't antagonise each other either. They can jog along amicably for quite a while but long-term they may find they each want more than the other can provide.

Pig with Goat

Happy-go-lucky Pig and laid-back Goat make a good pair. They hate to stir up trouble and always look for a peaceful solution to any challenge. Ideally, they'd avoid the challenge altogether. They could be very contented together as long as Pig's spending and Goat's inability to deal with finances doesn't get them into trouble.

Pig with Monkey

On the surface, these two might seem an unlikely couple. Yet Pig enjoys Monkey's fun and humour while Monkey is happy to be admired uncritically. What's more, Monkey's inventive mind can solve any difficulties caused by Pig's spending and since Monkey can't resist a challenge, the opportunity to retrain Pig or at least find a way to obtain purchases cheaper could help the relationship last.

Pig with Rooster

These two might seem an unlikely couple – modest Pig with extrovert Rooster. Yet Pig has no need or wish to crow, and can see the vulnerable character that lurks beneath Rooster's fine feathers. While Rooster responds to Pig's kindness and undemanding nature. As long as Rooster doesn't get bored, this can be a contented relationship.

Pig with Dog

In the outside world, the dog and the pig can get along well together; in fact, pigs, being intelligent creatures, can do many of the things dogs can do, so it's not surprising this zodiac pair make a good couple. Good natured Pig is uncomplicated and fair-minded which suits Dog perfectly. Also, Pig brings out Dog's playful side – which delights Pig who's always keen to have a playmate. A happy relationship involving many restaurants.

Pig Love 2020 Style

Great news Pig – whether single or spoken for, it looks like a very loved-up year for you. The Rat has always found you decidedly cute and appealing, and this year an aura of desirability will cling to you as a result.

To be fair this is not unusual. The Pig is a sexy, sensuous sign and even those Pigs not blessed with conventional good looks have no trouble attracting smitten admirers.

Single Pigs will probably have to pick and choose in 2020 because so many other signs will fall for their charms. Actually, good-natured Pigs have no objection to running several relationships at the same time but for some reason their prospective partners tend to make a fuss about this!

It seems a shame to have to let some promising loves go, but it looks like you'll just have to resolve not to be greedy Pig.

And you could very well find your soul mate this year. As we've seen, there is a big celebration coming up for typical Pigs in 2020 – it could even be your own wedding.

Attached Pigs can look forward to some long spells of domestic bliss. Just watch out for arguments caused by jealousy. There's a chance a blast from the past could return without warning and cause friction in the Pig home.

You may have to ask yourself, Pig, whether it's really all over or whether you still retain some feelings for this individual. Unsurprisingly, this dilemma is unlikely to go down well with your other half, so proceed with care. But whatever you decide in the end, love will find a way.

Secrets of Success in 2020

Unlike many signs, you don't measure success by fancy titles at work and the latest designer clothes. The Pig mainly wants to be happy and have fun. If the Pig is enjoying life, that's success enough.

So, this year, typical Pigs will be even more successful than last. Why? Well the birth year pressure has reduced several notches, the social scene is buzzing, the Pig love-life is sizzling, and even work is going well. A pay rise is likely. What's not to like?

The only pitfall that could trip your progress, Pig, is too much reckless spending, plus your love of gossip.

Keep a firm grip on your credit card and remind yourself that it really is money. Then resist the temptation to pass on every juicy titbit of news that comes your way.

Sociable Pigs love to chat. They'll happily chat to anyone and such is their friendly, sympathetic manner, they often end up being confided in. The trouble is, without for one moment meaning any harm, many Pigs see nothing wrong in sharing the info with everyone else they meet.

This year there will be consequences, Pig, and you won't like them. So be discreet. Bite your lip and you'll sail through the year.

The Pig Year at a Glance

January – Your fortunes will build as the year goes on. No need to rush. Take your time over decisions.

February – A sociable month with many informal get-togethers.

March – A friend has a good idea you can help with.

April – Finances are improving. Your career is looking up but beware of back-stabbers.

May – Tempting offers surround you. You may even be looking at new homes.

June – You love mid-summer. It's the time to party. You're in the mood to organise something spectacular.

July – You're on a roll. Money flows in, your projects are going well.

August – You're ready for adventure. Check out the holiday brochures and pick something unexpected.

September – You're Ms or Mr Popularity right now. Rock your finest and make the most of things.

October – Oops… after so much partying, it's time to concentrate on work.

November – Beware. This is your danger month for gossip. Zip your lip, and stay out of trouble.

December – Phew. Relax again. Everyone's lightening up and you can enjoy the festive season as only a true Pig can.

Lucky Colours 2020: Yellow, Grey, Brown

Lucky Numbers 2020: 1,5,9

CHAPTER 14: BUT THEN THERE'S SO MUCH MORE TO YOU

So now you know your animal sign, but possibly you're thinking – okay, but how can everyone born in the same year as me have the same personality as me?

You've only got to think back to your class at school, full of children the same age as you, to know this can't be true. And you're absolutely right. What's more, Chinese astrologers agree with you. For this reason, in Chinese astrology, your birth year is only the beginning. The month you were born and the hour of your birth are also ruled by the twelve zodiac animals – and not necessarily the same animal that rules your birth year.

These other animals then go on to modify the qualities of your basic year personality. So someone born in an extrovert Tiger year but at the time of day ruled by the quieter Ox, and in the month of the softly spoken Snake, for instance, would very likely find their risk-taking Tiger qualities much toned down and enhanced by a few other calmer, more subtle traits.

By combining these three important influences, you get a much more accurate and detailed picture of the complex and unique person you really are. These calculations lead to so many permutations it soon becomes clear how people born in the same year can share various similarities, yet still remain quite different from each other.

What's more, the other animals linked to your date of birth can also have a bearing on how successful you will be in any year and how well you get on with people from other signs. Traditionally, the Horse and the Rabbit don't get on well together, for instance, so you'd expect two people born in these years to be unlikely to end up good friends. Yet if both individuals had other compatible signs in their charts, they could find themselves surprisingly warming to each other.

This is how it works:

Your Outer Animal – (Birth Year | Creates Your First Impression)

You're probably completely unaware of it, but when people meet you for the first time, they will sense the qualities represented by the animal that ruled your birth year. Your Outer Animal and its personality influence the way you appear to the outside world. Your Outer animal is your public face. You may not feel the least bit like this creature deep down, and you may wonder why nobody seems to understand the real you. Why is it that people always seem to underestimate you, or perhaps overestimate you, you may ask yourself frequently. The reason is that you just can't help giving the impression of your birth-year animal and people will tend to see you and think of you in this way – especially if they themselves were born in other years.

Your Inner Animal – (Birth Month | The Private You)

Your Inner Animal is the animal that rules the month in which you were born. The personality of this creature tells you a lot about how you feel inside, what motivates you, and how you tend to live your life. When you're out in the world and want to present yourself in the best light, it's easy for you to project the finest talents of your birth-year animal. You've got them at your fingertips. But at home, with no one you need to impress, your Inner Animal comes to the fore. You can kick back and relax. You may find you have abilities and interests that no one at work would ever guess. Only your closest friends and loved ones are likely to get to know your Inner Animal.

By now you know your Outer Animal so you can move on to find your Inner Animal from the chart below:

Month of Birth - Your Inner Animal

January – the Ox

February – the Tiger

March – the Rabbit

April – the Dragon

May – the Snake

June – the Horse

July – the Goat

August – the Monkey

September – the Rooster

October – the Dog

November – the Pig

December – the Rat

Your Secret Animal – (Birth Hour | The Still, Small Voice Within)

Your secret animal rules the time you were born. Each 24-hour period is divided into 12, two-hour time-slots and each slot is believed to be ruled by a particular animal. This animal represents the deepest, most secret part of you. It's possibly the most intimate, individual part of you as it marks the moment you first entered the world and became 'you'. This animal is possibly your conscience and your inspiration. It might represent qualities you'd like to have or sometimes fail to live up to. Chances are, no one else will ever meet your Secret Animal.

For your Secret Animal check out the time of your birth:

Hours of Birth – Your Secret Animal

1 am – 3 am – the Ox

3 am – 5 am – the Tiger

5 am – 7 am – the Rabbit

7 am – 9 am – the Dragon

9 am – 11 am – the Snake

11 am – 1.00 pm – the Horse

1.00 pm – 3.00 pm – the Goat

3.00 pm – 5.00 pm – the Monkey

5.00 pm – 7.00 pm – the Rooster

7.00 pm – 9.00 pm – the Dog

9.00 pm – 11.00 pm – the Pig

11.00 pm – 1.00 am – the Rat

When you've found your other animals, go back to the previous chapters and read the sections on those particular signs. You may well discover talents and traits that you recognise immediately as belonging to you in addition to those mentioned in your birth year. It could also be that your Inner Animal or your Secret Animal is the same as your Year animal. A Dragon born at 8 am in the morning, for instance, will be a secret Dragon inside as well as outside, because the hours between 7 am and 9 am are ruled by the Dragon.

When this happens, it suggests that the positive and the less positive attributes of the Dragon will be held in harmony, so this particular Dragon ends up being very well balanced.

You might also like to look at your new animal's compatibility with other signs and see where you might be able to widen your circle of friends and improve your love life.

CHAPTER 15: IN YOUR ELEMENT

There's no doubt about it, Chinese astrology has many layers. But then we all recognise that we have many facets to our personalities, too. We are all more complicated than we might first appear. And more unique, as well.

It turns out that even people who share the same Birth Year sign are not identical to people with the same sign but born in different years. A Rabbit born in 1963, for instance, will express their Rabbit personality in a slightly different way to a Rabbit born in 1975. This is not simply down to the influence of the other animals in their chart, it's because each year is also believed to be ruled by one of the five Chinese 'elements', as well as the year animal.

These elements are known as Water, Wood, Fire, Earth, and Metal.

Each element is thought to contain special qualities which are bestowed onto people born in the year it ruled, in addition to the qualities of their animal sign.

Since there are 12 signs endlessly rotating, and five elements, the same animal and element pairing only recurs once every 60 years. Which is why babies born in this 2020 year of the Golden Rat are unlikely to grow up remembering much about other Metal Rats from the previous generation. Those senior Rats will already be 60 years old when the new kittens or pups are born.

In years gone by, when life expectancy was much lower, the chances are there would only ever be one generation of a particular combined sign and element alive in the world at a time.

Find Your Element from the Chart Below:

The 1920s

5 February 1924 – 24 January 1925 | RAT | WOOD

25 January 1925 – 12 February 1926 | OX | WOOD

13 February 1926 – 1 February 1927 | TIGER | FIRE

2 February 1927 – 22 January 1928 | RABBIT | FIRE

23 January 1928 – 9 February 1929 | DRAGON | EARTH

10 February 1929 – 29 January 1930 | SNAKE | EARTH

The 1930s

30 January 1930 – 16 February 1931 | HORSE | METAL

17 February 1931 – 5 February 1932 | GOAT | METAL

6 February 1932 – 25 January 1933 | MONKEY | WATER

26 January 1933 – 13 February 1934 | ROOSTER | WATER

14 February 1934 – 3 February 1935 | DOG | WOOD

4 February 1935 – 23 January 1936 | PIG | WOOD

24 January 1936 – 10 February 1937 | RAT | FIRE

11 February 1937 – 30 January 1938 | OX | FIRE

31 January 1938 – 18 February 1939 | TIGER | EARTH

19 February 1939 – 7 February 1940 | RABBIT | EARTH

The 1940s

8 February 1940 – 26 January 1941 | DRAGON | METAL

27 January 1941 – 14 February 1942 | SNAKE | METAL

15 February 1942 – 4 February 1943 | HORSE | WATER

5 February 1943 – 24 January 1944 | GOAT | WATER

25 January 1944 – 12 February 1945 | MONKEY | WOOD

13 February 1945 – 1 February 1946 | ROOSTER | WOOD

2 February 1946 – 21 January 1947 | DOG | FIRE

22 January 1947 – 9 February 1948 | PIG | FIRE

10 February 1948 – 28 January 1949 | RAT | EARTH

29 January 1949 – 16 February 1950 | OX | EARTH

The 1950s

17 February 1950 – 5 February 1951 | TIGER | METAL

6 February 1951 – 26 January 1952 | RABBIT | METAL

27 January 1952 – 13 February 1953 | DRAGON | WATER

14 February 1953 – 2 February 1954 | SNAKE | WATER

3 February 1954 – 23 January 1955 | HORSE | WOOD

24 January 1955 – 11 February 1956 | GOAT | WOOD

12 February 1956 – 30 January 1957 | MONKEY | FIRE

31 January 1957 – 17 February 1958 | ROOSTER | FIRE

18 February 1958 – 7 February 1959 | DOG | EARTH

8 February 1959 – 27 January 1960 | PIG | EARTH

The 1960s

28 January 1960 – 14 February 1961 | RAT | METAL

15 February 1961 – 4 February 1962 | OX | METAL

5 February 1962 – 24 January 1963 | TIGER | WATER

25 January 1963 – 12 February 1964 | RABBIT | WATER

13 February 1964 – 1 February 1965 | DRAGON | WOOD

2 February 1965 – 20 January 1966 | SNAKE | WOOD

21 January 1966 – 8 February 1967 | HORSE | FIRE

9 February 1967 – 29 January 1968 | GOAT | FIRE

30 January 1968 – 16 February 1969 | MONKEY | EARTH

17 February 1969 – 5 February 1970 | ROOSTER | EARTH

The 1970s

6 February 1970 – 26 January 1971 | DOG | METAL

27 January 1971 – 14 February 1972 | PIG | METAL

15 February 1972 – 2 February 1973 | RAT | WATER

3 February 1973 – 22 January 1974 | OX | WATER

23 January 1974 – 10 February 1975 | TIGER | WOOD

11 February 1975 – 30 January 1976 | RABBIT | WOOD

31 January 1976 – 17 February 1977 | DRAGON | FIRE

18 February 1977 – 6 February 1978 | SNAKE | FIRE

7 February 1978 – 27 January 1979 | HORSE | EARTH

28 January 1979 – 15 February 1980 | GOAT | EARTH

The 1980s

16 February 1980 – 4 February 1981 | MONKEY | METAL

5 February 1981 – 24 January 1982 | ROOSTER | METAL

25 January 1982 – 12 February 1983 | DOG | WATER

13 February 1983 – 1 February 1984 | PIG | WATER

2 February 1984 – 19 February 1985 | RAT | WOOD

20 February 1985 – 8 February 1986 | OX | WOOD

9 February 1986 – 28 January 1987 | TIGER | FIRE

29 January 1987 – 16 February 1988 | RABBIT | FIRE

17 February 1988 – 5 February 1989 | DRAGON | EARTH

6 February 1989 – 26 January 1990 | SNAKE | EARTH

The 1990s

27 January 1990 – 14 February 1991 | HORSE | METAL

15 February 1991 – 3 February 1992 | GOAT | METAL

4 February 1992 – 22 January 1993 | MONKEY | WATER

23 January 1993 – 9 February 1994 | ROOSTER | WATER

10 February 1994 – 30 January 1995 | DOG | WOOD

31 January 1995 – 18 February 1996 | PIG | WOOD

19 February 1996 – 7 February 1997 | RAT | FIRE

8 February 1997 – 27 January 1998 | OX | FIRE

28 January 1998 – 5 February 1999 | TIGER | EARTH

6 February 1999 – 4 February 2000 | RABBIT | EARTH

The 2000s

5 February 2000 – 23 January 2001 | DRAGON | METAL

24 January 2001 – 11 February 2002 | SNAKE | METAL

12 February 2002 – 31 January 2003 | HORSE | WATER

1 February 2003 – 21 January 2004 | GOAT | WATER

22 January 2004 – 8 February 2005 | MONKEY | WOOD

9 February 2005 – 28 January 2006 | ROOSTER | WOOD

29 January 2006 – 17 February 2007 | DOG | FIRE

18 February 2007 – 6 February 2008 | PIG | FIRE

7 February 2008 – 25 January 2009 | RAT | EARTH

26 January 2009 – 13 February 2010 | OX | EARTH

The 2010s

14 February 2010 – 2 February 2011 | TIGER | METAL

3 February 2011 – 22 January 2012 | RABBIT | METAL

23 January 2012 – 9 February 2013 | DRAGON | WATER

10 February 2013 – 30 January 2014 | SNAKE | WATER

31 January 2014 – 18 February 2015 | HORSE | WOOD

19 February 2015 – 7 February 2016 | GOAT | WOOD

8 February 2016 – 27 January 2017 | MONKEY | FIRE

28 January 2017 – 15 February 2018 | ROOSTER | FIRE

16 February 2018 – 4 February 2019 | DOG | EARTH

5 February 2019 – 24 January 2020 | PIG | EARTH

The 2020s

25 January 2020 – 11 February 2021 | RAT | METAL

12 February 2021 – 1 February 2022 | OX | METAL

2 February 2022 – 21 January 2023 | TIGER | WATER

22 January 2023 – 9 February 2024 | RABBIT | WATER

10 February 2024 – 28 January 2025 | DRAGON | WOOD

29 January 2025 – 16 February 2026 | SNAKE | WOOD

17 February 2026 – 5 February 2027 | HORSE | FIRE

6 February 2027 – 25 January 2028 | GOAT | FIRE

26 January 2028 – 12 February 2029 | MONKEY | EARTH

13 February 2029 – 2 February 2030 | ROOSTER | EARTH

You may have noticed that the 'natural' basic element of your sign is not necessarily the same as the element of the year you were born. Don't worry about this. The element of your birth year takes precedence, though you could also read the qualities assigned to the natural element as well, as these will be relevant to your personality but to a lesser degree.

Metal

Metal is the element associated in China with gold and wealth. So if you are a Metal child, you will be very good at accumulating money. The Metal individual is ambitious, even if their animal sign is not particularly career-minded. The Metal-born version of an unworldly sign will still somehow have an eye for a bargain or a good investment; they'll manage to buy at the right time when prices are low and be moved to sell just as the price is peaking. If they want to get rid of unwanted items, they'll potter along to a car boot sale and without appearing to try, somehow make a killing, selling the lot while stalls around them struggle for attention. Career-minded signs with the element Metal have to be careful they don't overdo things. They have a tendency to become workaholics. Wealth will certainly flow, but it could be at the expense of family harmony and social life.

The element of Metal adds power, drive, and tenacity to whatever sign it influences so if you were born in a Metal year you'll never lack cash for long.

Water

Water is the element associated with communication, creativity, and the emotions. Water has a knack of flowing around obstacles, finding routes that are not obvious to the naked eye and seeping into the smallest cracks. So if you're a Water child, you'll be very good at getting what you want in an oblique, unchallenging way. You are one of nature's lateral thinkers. You are also wonderful with people. You're sympathetic, empathetic, and can always find the right words at the right time. You can also be highly persuasive, but in such a subtle way nobody notices your influence or input. They think the whole thing was their own idea.

People born in Water years are very creative and extremely intuitive. They don't know where their inspiration comes from, but somehow ideas just pour into their brains. Many artists were born in Water years.

Animal signs that are normally regarded as a little impatient and tactless have their rough edges smoothed when they appear in a Water year. People born in these years will be more diplomatic, artistic, and amiable than other versions of their fellow signs. And if you were born in a naturally sensitive, emotional sign, in a Water year, you'll be so intuitive you're probably psychic. Yet just as water can fall as gentle nurturing rain, or a raging destructive flood, so Water types need to take care not to let their emotions run away with them or to allow themselves to use their persuasive skills to be too manipulative.

Wood

Wood is the element associated with growth and expansion. In Chinese astrology, Wood doesn't primarily refer to the inert variety used to make floorboards and furniture, it represents living, flourishing trees and smaller plants, all pushing out of the earth and growing towards the sky.

Wood is represented by the colour green, not brown. If you're a Wood child, you're likely to be honest, generous, and friendly. You think BIG and like to be involved in numerous projects, often at the same time.

Wood people are practical yet imaginative and able to enlist the support of others simply by the sincerity and enthusiasm with which they tackle their plans. Yet even though they're always busy with a project, they somehow radiate calm, stability, and confidence. There's a sense of the timeless serenity of a big old tree about Wood people. Other signs instinctively trust them and look to them for guidance.

Animal signs that could be prone to nervousness or impulsive behaviour tend to be calmer and more productive in Wood year versions, while signs whose natural element is also Wood could well end up leaders of vast teams or business empires. Wood people tend to sail smoothly through life, but they must guard against becoming either stubborn or unyielding as they grow older or alternatively, saying 'yes' to every new plan and overextending themselves.

Fire

Fire is the element associated with dynamism, strength, and persistence. Fire demands action, movement, and expansion. It also creates a huge amount of heat. Fire is precious when it warms our homes and cooks our food, and it possesses a savage beauty that's endlessly fascinating. Yet it's also highly dangerous and destructive if it gets out of control. Something of this ambivalent quality is evident in Fire children.

People born in Fire years tend to be immensely attractive, magnetic types. Other signs are drawn to them. Yet there is always a hint of danger, of unpredictability, about them. You never know quite where you are with a Fire year sign and in a way, this is part of their fascination.

People born in Fire years like to get things done. They are extroverted and bold and impatient for action. They are brilliant at getting things started and energising people and projects. Quieter signs born in a Fire year are more dynamic, outspoken, and energetic than their fellow sign cousins, while extrovert signs positively blaze with exuberance and confidence when Fire is added to the mix.

People born in Fire years will always be noticed, but they should try to remember they tend to be impatient and impulsive. Develop a habit of pausing to take a deep breath to consider things, before rushing in, and you won't get burned.

Earth

Earth is the element associated with patience, stability, and practicality. This may not sound exciting but, in Chinese astrology, Earth is at the centre of everything: the heart of the planet. Earth year children are strong, hardworking personalities. They will persist with a task if it's worthwhile and never give up until it's complete. They create structure and balance, and they have very nurturing instincts.

Women born in Earth years make wonderful mothers, and if they're not mothering actual children, they'll be mothering their colleagues at work, or their friends and relatives, while also filling their homes with houseplants and raising vegetables in the garden if at all possible.

Other signs like being around Earth types as they exude a sense of security. Earth people don't like change, and they strive to keep their lives settled and harmonious. They are deeply kind and caring and immensely honest. Tact is not one of their strong points, however. They will always say what they think, so if you don't want the unvarnished truth, better not to ask!

Earth lends patience and stability to the more flighty, over-emotional signs, and rock solid integrity to the others. Earth people will be sought-after in whatever field they choose to enter, but they must take care not to become too stubborn. Make a point of seeking out and listening to a wide range of varying opinions before setting a decision in stone.

Yin and Yang

As you looked down the table of years and elements, you may have noticed that the elements came in pairs. Each element was repeated the following year. If the Monkey was Water one year, it would be followed immediately the next year by the Rooster, also Water.

This is because of Yin and Yang – the mysterious but vital forces that, in Chinese philosophy, are believed to control the planet and probably the whole universe. They can be thought of as positive and negative, light and dark, masculine and feminine, night and day, etc. but the important point is that everything is either Yin or Yang; the two forces complement each other and both are equally important because only together do they make up the whole. For peace and harmony to be achieved, both forces need to be in balance.

Each of the animal signs is believed to be either Yin or Yang and because of the need for balance and harmony, they alternate through the years. Six of the 12 signs are Yin and six are Yang and since Yang represents extrovert, dominant energy, the Yang sign is first, followed by the Yin sign which represents quiet, passive force. A Yang sign is always followed by a Yin sign throughout the cycle.

The Yang signs are:

Rat

Tiger

Dragon

Horse

Monkey

Dog

The Yin Signs are

Ox

Rabbit

Snake

Goat

Rooster

Pig

Although Yang is seen as a masculine energy, and Yin a feminine energy, in reality, whether you are male or female, everyone has a mixture of Yin and Yang within them. If you need to know, quickly, whether your sign is Yin or Yang just check your birth year. If it ends in an even number (or 0) your sign is Yang. If it ends in an odd number, your sign is Yin.

In general, Yang signs tend to be extrovert, action-oriented types while Yin signs are gentler, more thoughtful, and patient.

So, as balance is essential when an element controls a period of time, it needs to express itself in its stronger Yang form in a Yang year as well as in its gentler Yin form in a Yin year, to be complete.

That's why this year of the Metal Rat (Yang) will be followed next year in 2021 by the Metal Ox (Yin) before the Metal element is complete and the stage is set for Water in 2022.

But why do elements have two forms? It's to take into account the great variations in strength encompassed by an element. The difference between a candle flame and a raging inferno – both belonging to Fire; or a great oak tree and a little seedling – both belonging to the Wood element.

In Yang years, the influence of the ruling element will be particularly strong.

Friendly Elements

Just as some signs get on well together and others don't, so some elements work well together while others don't. These are the elements that exist in harmony:

METAL likes EARTH and WATER

WATER likes METAL and WOOD

WOOD likes WATER and FIRE

FIRE likes WOOD and EARTH

EARTH likes FIRE and METAL

The reason for these friendly partnerships is believed to be the natural, productive cycle. Water nourishes Wood and makes plants grow, Wood provides fuel for Fire, Fire produces ash which is a type of Earth, Earth can be melted or mined to produce Metal while Metal contains or carries Water in a bucket.

Unfriendly Elements

But since everything has to be in balance, all the friendly elements are opposed by the same number of unfriendly elements. These are the elements that are not in harmony:

METAL dislikes WOOD and FIRE

WATER dislikes FIRE and EARTH

WOOD dislikes EARTH and METAL

FIRE dislikes METAL and WATER

EARTH dislikes WOOD and WATER

The reason some elements don't get on is down to the destructive cycle which is: Water puts out Fire and is absorbed by Earth, Wood breaks up Earth (with its strong roots) and is harmed by Metal tools, Metal is melted by fire and can cut down Wood.

So if someone just seems to rub you up the wrong way, for no logical reason, it could be that your elements clash.

CHAPTER 16: CREATE A WONDERFUL YEAR

By now, you should have got a pretty good idea of the main influences on your life and personality, according to Chinese astrology. But how is 2020 going to shape up for you? Well, that largely depends on how cleverly you play your hand.

The Year of the Rat is traditionally a fast-paced, exciting year bringing new beginnings and fresh opportunities for all the signs. Yet some signs will find the conditions ahead more comfortable than others. Zodiac creatures that prefer to think things over carefully, before making a move, can find it more difficult to adapt to the bracing Rat energy. Yet, as long as you're prepared – and you know what you might be up against – you can develop plans to ride those waves like a world-class surfer.

Sit back and rely on good fortune alone, because it's a terrific year for your sign, and you could snatch failure from the jaws of success. Navigate any stormy seas with skill and foresight if it's not such a sunny year for your sign, and you'll sail on to fulfil your dreams. This is always true in any year, but *doubly* so when Rat's in charge. Above all, the Rat rewards genuine effort and can't abide laziness. So no matter what zodiac sign you were born under, 'Rat year energy' will help you if you help yourself.

The future is not set in stone.

Chinese astrology is used very much like a weather forecast, so that you can check out the likely conditions you'll encounter on your journey and plan your route and equipment accordingly. Some signs might need a parasol and sandals; while others, stout walking boots and rain-gear. Yet, properly prepared, both will end up in a good place at the end of the trip.

Finally, it's said that if you feel another sign has a much better outlook than you this year, you can carry a small symbol of that animal with you (in the form of a piece of jewellery, perhaps, or a tiny charm in your pocket or bag) and their good luck will rub off on you. Does it work? For some, maybe, but there's certainly no harm in trying.

Other Books from Bennion Kearny

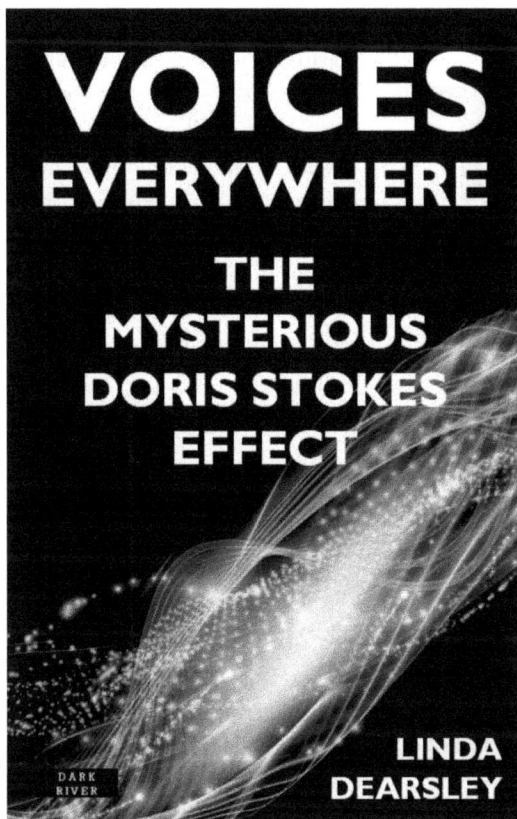

VOICES EVERYWHERE

THE MYSTERIOUS DORIS STOKES EFFECT

LINDA DEARSLEY

DARK RIVER

Linda Dearsley was Doris Stokes' ghost.

Well, more accurately, she was the ghost-writer for Doris Stokes and worked with her for 10 years to produce 7 books, detailing the great lady's life.

In Voices Everywhere, Linda shines a light on her time working with Doris, right from the very early days when Doris was doing private readings in her Fulham flat, to filling the London Palladium and Barbican night after night, to subsequent fame outside the UK. Throughout all this, Doris Stokes never became anyone other than who she was: a kind, generous, and down-to-earth woman with an extraordinary gift, and a fondness for a nice cup of tea. January 6th, 2020, would have been Doris' 100th birthday.

Following Doris' death, Linda chronicles how cynics tried to torpedo the Stokes legacy with accusations of cheating and dishonesty, but how those closest to Doris never believed she was anything other than genuine.

In turn, as the months and years rolled by, more and more intriguing people crossed Linda's path, each with their own unexplainable power, and Doris never seemed far away. From the palmist who saw pictures in people's hands, to the couple whose marriage was predicted by Doris, and the woman who believes she captures departed spirits on camera – the mysterious world of the paranormal, and Doris Stokes' place within it, continues to unfold.

TAROT
IN 5 MINUTES

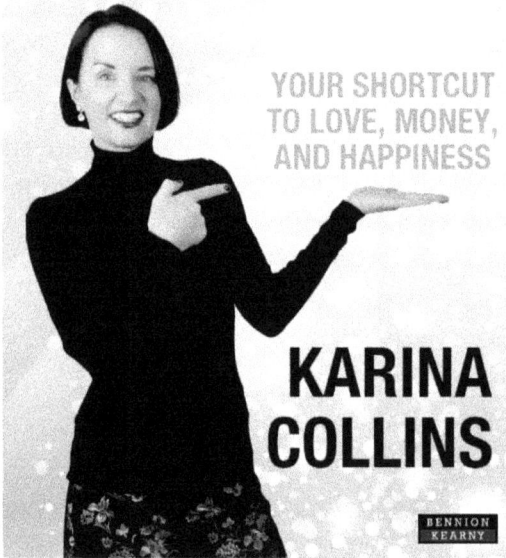

YOUR SHORTCUT
TO LOVE, MONEY,
AND HAPPINESS

KARINA
COLLINS

BENNION
KEARNY

Karina Collins is an acclaimed Tarot reader who has helped people, from all walks of life, to better understand their lives' journeys. Now, she is on a mission to help you take control of your life – through the power of Tarot – to better explore and understand your purpose and destiny.

Do you have questions about now and your future? Perhaps about making more money, or whether love is on the horizon, or whether you will become happier? Do you want to steer your life in a direction that brings success, pleasure, and fulfilment? Well, Tarot is a means to help you do exactly that! Used for centuries, it provides a powerful tool for unlocking knowledge, divining the future, and delivering shortcuts to the lives we desire.

In this full-colour book, Karina provides explanations and insights into the full 78-card Tarot deck, how to phrase questions most effectively, real-world sample readings, why seemingly scary cards represent opportunities for growth and triumph, and more.

"...a fascinating book... an excellent introduction to the different aspects of parapsychology. Lumsden writes with wit and insight."
Tucson Citizen

BENNION KEARNY

THE HIDDEN WHISPER

JJ LUMSDEN

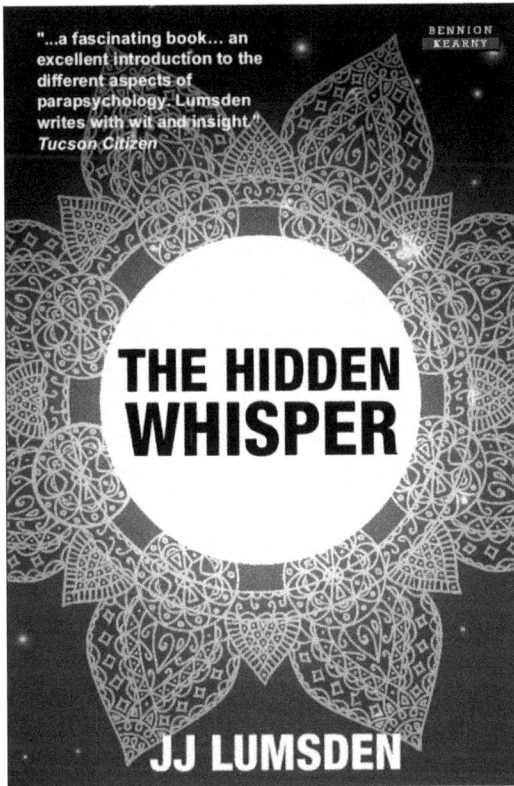

A paranormal puzzle smoulders in the desert heat of southern Arizona. At the home of Jack and Chloe Monroe, a written message "Leave Now" appears then disappears, a candle in an empty room mysteriously lights itself, and – most enigmatically – an unidentifiable ethereal whisper begins to permeate the house. What was once simply strange now feels sinister. What once seemed a curiosity now seems terrifying.

Dr. Luke Jackson, a British Parapsychologist visiting family nearby, is asked to investigate and quickly finds himself drawn deeper into the series of unexplained events. Time is against him. He has just one week to understand and resolve the poltergeist case before he must depart Arizona.

The Hidden Whisper is the acclaimed paranormal thriller, written by real-life parapsychologist Dr. JJ Lumsden, which offers a rare opportunity to enter the intriguing world of parapsychology through the eyes of Luke Jackson. The fictional narrative is combined with extensive endnotes and references that cover Extra Sensory Perception, Psychokinesis, Haunts, Poltergeists, Out of Body Experiences, and more. If you thought parapsychology was like Ghostbusters – think again...

"This book works on many levels, an excellent introduction to the concepts current in the field of parapsychology... at best you may learn something new, and at worst you'll have read a witty and well-written paranormal detective story" Parascience.

www.BennionKearny.com/paranormal

Lightning Source UK Ltd.
Milton Keynes UK
UKHW020621040220
358132UK00012B/805

9 781911 121848